Open

Heart
Therapy

Robert Steven Mandel

Open
Heart
Therapy

Celestial Arts
Berkeley, California

Celestial Arts
P.O. Box 7327
Berkeley, CA 94707

First Printing, 1984

Cover art: Irv Klein
Cover design: Irv Klein
Interior design: Paul Quin/QR
Interior illustrations: Deborah Russell/QR
Typography: HMS Typography, Inc.

Made in the United States of America

Library of Congress Catalog Number: 84-045360
ISBN: 0-89087-408-5

1   2   3   4   5   6 — 88   87   86   85   84

Dedication

To my beloved wife Mallie and the children, Kim and Susanna, that you brought into my heart.

Words cannot even begin to describe the gratitude I feel for all you have given me and all you have allowed me to give you.

I love you and I will never leave you!

Acknowledgments

Mom, for showing me there is an infinite reservoir of love.

Dad, for supporting me in taking chances and risking failure.

Bryna, for your unconditional love, support and creative inspiration.

Sondra, for creating the Loving Relationships Training and for your unwavering support in my going for it.

Leonard, for leading me to my breath and allowing my breath to lead me.

Robert, for being the brother I never had.

Doreen, for your joy, enthusiasm, constant friendship and devotion to family.

Peter, for caring so deeply and teaching me my love is good enough.

Diane, for showing me that love can be earth, air, fire or water.

Fred, for being a shining mirror in which to perfect myself.

Steven, for helping me to choose my freedom.

Bobby, for inspiring me to fear forward.

Wendy, for absolutely always being there.

Larry, for Open Heart Productions.

and, to my family of friends everywhere,

Thank you!

Thank you!

Thank you!

This book is for everyone.

> If you've ever been shut down, shut up, shut out or shut off;
> if you've ever held back, held in, held out or held off;
> if you weren't held enough as a child;
> if you want to be held right now;
> if you're holding on to old pain;
> if your love life's on hold;
> this book is for you!
>
> If you're hopeless about love,
> feel like a victim,
> or had never been born,
> this book is for you!
>
> If you wonder whether it's really better to have loved and lost than
> never to have loved at all;
> if you've loved and lost and want to recapture romance;
> if your heart is numb, empty and longing;
> if love is a luxury you think you can't afford;
> if love seems illogical;
> if it doesn't make a difference because you think the world is
> doomed;
> if all options seem unacceptable;
> if you want to give up but don't know how to surrender;
> if you've tasted the divine elixir of love and now feel ready to feast;
> this book is for you!
>
> This book is for everyone.
>
> It's safe to love again!

Table of Contents

Note to the Reader

This is a self-help book. In addition to the philosophy and psychology of love presented here, there are numerous "implants" and "by-passes" for you to do. The more you do your homework, the more these love lessons will work for you.

An "implant" is really a seed of transformation—a specific positive attitude that you plant in your subconscious mind through repetition in order to de-program negative patterns and replace them with positive ones. The result, if used properly, is a basic attitudinal change which affects your entire life. Sometimes implants are called *affirmations*.

A "by-pass" is an operation you perform on your own mind. It is a simple, safe structure in which you can locate thoughts, feelings and "stuck" points for the purpose of overcoming them. A by-pass can also be used for positive re-enforcement. While there are no panaceas prescribed in this book, there are shortcuts to an easier, happier life. A bypass is a way to cut your mind off at the pass—before it ambushes you later on!

Foreword: A Tribute to Bob

What kind of person could be the director of the Loving Relationships Training for the world?

Someone who would write a book called Open Heart Therapy.

Someone who would be my equal.

Someone I could trust forever in every cell of my body.

Someone who could and would make the same decision I would have made or better in case I was abroad or not available.

Someone who would be an inspiration of total love, total openness, total honesty, total surrender and totally giving.

Someone who was in a good relationship and demonstrating it to the world, always living the principles.

Someone whose own case was not in the way of his work

Someone who understands what is really going on with personal relationships, business and staff relationships and relationships between countries.

Someone who could create and run spiritual families and keep them growing.

Someone who is completely dedicated to the spiritual life who understands that work is worship.

Someone who has the energy, the fortitude and the vision to handle anything that could come up.

I needed, quite frankly, someone who is a miracle, someone like Bob Mandel.

I acknowledge you, Bob, for this book and for all your work in the world. And I agree with Robert Rosellini's acknowledgment of you: You have mastered leadership without domination.

Thank you,
Sondra Ray

Chapter I

The Dilemma
of love

The dilemma of love is as simple as it is baffling.

How can we trust love when love has proven so untrustworthy in the past? How can we put our faith in an experience that we fear is only an illusion, a dream from which we are doomed to awaken? How can we overcome cynicism, the last refuge of the romantics?

How can we trust others to be there for us when in the past we were disappointed? How can we trust ourselves to be there for others when we've suffered so many changes of heart? How can we have relationships that are neither brief passionate romances nor long-drawn-out struggles? How can we make love last? How can we resolve the pleasure of love with the pain love always seems to imply—the helplessness, the struggle, the control, the guilt, the disapproval? Is love ever worth the cost? Is the taste of the eternal worth biting the hook of our apparent mortality? Or is love just a momentary respite between birth and death, a sweet joke on the way to the gallows?

Look at the great fictional lovers of the past. Tristan and Isolde, Romeo and Juliet. The premise underlying their love stories showed romantic love to be, not only socially unacceptable, but also utterly futile in this lifetime. Romance is a great fiction, an escapist fantasy, a temporary relief from "reality."

And yet life without love seems hardly worth the effort. When we seek to translate the quest for love into more "practical" terms, we delude ourselves further. The lust for money, power and sexual conquest is an empty quest, rendering the seeker frustrated and empty at the core.

On the other hand, the attempt to reduce love to a socially viable way of life is usually tedious and boring. Conventional marriage seems a failure by most standards. Look at the soaring divorce rate. Marriage, originally intended as a spiritual union, is now diminished to a social convenience, a family tradition, a legal contract, a travesty of spirit! And bonding with a mate "'til death do us part" has a built-in doomsday factor that amplifies the fear of loss it seeks to overcome. Divorce then becomes a greater expression of life than wedlock. Who wants to be locked into another closed system? Rebels that we are, we kill love before love kills us.

The closed system not only dooms us in the long run, but also inhibits us every breath of the way. How can we surrender to greater love and pleasure when we're taught to conserve our resources, save for a rainy day? How can we live fully each day when we think our days are numbered?

We are victims of an energy crisis of our own fabrication. We are trapped in a crunch between eternal love and mortal fear. The result is a culture founded on hopelessness, fixated on fleeting fitness and addicted to cheap thrills. Truly, we live and love as though there were no tomorrow.

How do we overcome the dilemma of love, opening the door to the satisfaction we all know love can bring?

Chapter II

What is this crazy thing called Love?

This is a how-to-do-it book, make no mistake about it. The principles and procedures of open heart therapy, as outlined in this book, have worked for thousands of people. They can work for you.

Before we get to the hows, however, there are several whats, whys and wherefores worth examining.

What is love?

Our first knowledge of love is clearly in the womb, where an all-pervasive sense of well-being surrounds us, circulating through our body, nourishing and supporting our spiritual, mental and physical evolution.

In the first twelve weeks of prenatal development there is no umbilical cord to feed and oxygenate us. Up against the wall of the uterus, we grow rapidly during this period, nourished by our connection to mother, yet a miraculous new being growing, maturing, and fulfilling a destiny of its own! (There is an undeniable principle of life: Conception is almost always followed by rapid expansion and multiplication of energy—not only in the womb, but also in general. The time after we conceive a project is often the most exciting, energizing and productive period of growth.) We grow rapidly on pure life energy, our cells maturing and multiplying as is their nature.

After this preliminary stage, the umbilical cord forms and seems to supply all our wants and needs. Later in life, we often seek to re-create this umbilical attachment, compulsively at times, thinking that if only we could find a loving enough person, one who would selflessly sacrifice and take care of all our needs, we would once again feel that all-pervasive warmth and love we felt in the womb. This is a tragic miscalculation.

Love is more than having your needs met, though knowing your needs will be met is a prerequisite for love.

Having your needs met is a matter of survival. Having the love you desire and deserve is a matter of the quality of your life. When you know your survival is secure, then and only then can you freely turn your attention to the quality of your existence. Therein lies the birth of a healthy love life.

You don't have to be perfect to have a perfect relationship.

Another way of saying this is, once you know you can take care of yourself, joining forces with another self-sufficient individual represents a qualitative transformation of your life. Two independent people who agree to be mutually accountable to each other do so, not out of need, but out of a willingness to be supported, because they know support makes life easier and more pleasurable. They support each other's joy and aliveness, knowing full well that the happier your partner is, the easier it is for yourself. This is not necessarily love, but the way a healthy, loving relationship *looks*.

When we are born into a family, we quickly learn what love means to our parents. We receive a wide range of confusing and often contradictory messages concerning what is acceptable and what is objectionable behavior. It doesn't take long to discover what actions lead to smiles and what lead to frowns. Fairly early we conclude that love is something we earn from our parents through correct behavior. This pattern is often reinforced by religious education, where we learn how to earn God's love through good deeds. And so we either master the game of earning approval and avoiding disapproval, or we reject the entire procedure and become "bad" kids.

Is approval love? Certainly not. If the state of your heart always depends on what other people think of you, you are stuck in another closed system in which you must suppress yourself in order to win love. True love, in my opinion, is never based on self-suppression. Moreover, if you think you need the approval of others in order to survive, as seemed the case with your parents, you will become increasingly hostile and resentful towards those you want to like you (though you may hide these feelings behind a forced, socially acceptable smile). You always secretly hate the people you think you most need.

Draw *a vertical line down the middle of a blank page. At the top of the lefthand column, write "My mother's thoughts about love were..." At the top of the righthand column, write "My father's thoughts about love were..." Fill in both columns. Get a sense of what your parents' belief system on love was like, and begin to release the negative thoughts and embrace the positive ones more fully. See if you can do this without making your parents wrong. Notice what feelings come up for you.*

So the approval/disapproval game is just another version of the need/obligate game! I'll be perfectly nice to you and do whatever it takes to earn your love, then you'll be obligated to love me and maybe even think you need me to need you in order to survive. Of course, even if this game "works," it *won't* work, because you will loathe the object of your affection, wondering how anyone could be so stupid as to fall for such an act.

Love is much more than getting approval, though approval is often the natural result of a healthy love life.

Is love a hopeless mystery—something you "fall" into, hoping desperately that it will work out?

★ **Falling in love is the romantic's euphemism for infantile neediness.**

Falling in love is feeling that the hopeless longing to have someone take care of you forever might finally be fulfilled. Maybe you have finally found a parental substitute who will do the job so well you'll never have to grow up. The subconscious message in falling in love is "Catch me!"

Falling in love is the complete opposite to being in love. It makes great romantic novels, but in real life it's an expression of utter futility.

So what is this crazy thing called love?

Remembering those first few months in the womb, prior to umbilical attachments, prior to the need for approval, prior to the need for parental substitutes, we had an all-pervasive sense of well-being, of the life-supporting energy that sustains us: the feeling that we can grow and grow and grow without obstruction and that life is something that needs only itself.

☆ *What is love? Love is a powerful, life-supporting energy that flows through you when you flow through it. When flowing freely, this energy rejuvenates the cells of your body, making you "young at heart" once again.*

Love is a powerful, life-supporting energy that flows through you when you flow through it.

Only love heals. Doctors cure, medicine relieves unpleasant symptoms, but only love heals the core of a being. Doctors restore or replace damaged organs or limbs, but only love revitalizes the body, awakening numb cells to new spiritual vigor. Love is the supreme faith healer!

Love, then, is an experience of deep surrender. It requires faith and courage that the mortal mind cannot comprehend. Surrender is not submission to the will of another. *Surrender is yielding inwards to one's own feelings, vulnerabilities, intuition and aliveness—the hidden you, the unknown you. Surrender is falling in love with yourself!*

If you don't love yourself, who is supposed to do it for you?

How can you surrender to the unknown you if you fear the loss of your carefully constructed and very familiar ego self? How can you open up to love if your very foundation is self-defense? How can you let go if all you know is how to hold on? How can you relax into your heart energy if whenever you start to feel things intensely you automatically hold your breath and suppress energy? How can you tap your hidden resources and live life fully if you fear that the loss of the familiar walls you have created to ward off life means death?

It's safe to love again!

More hows. More contradictions. I'm telling you now that **the primary message of this book is simple!** *It's safe to love again!* But I'm also telling you that, due to a lifetime of conditioning, you will resist this message at every crossroads. That well-trained scientific voice in your mind will demand proof, evidence beyond a reasonable doubt. And the closer you come to dismantling the fortress that is your ego, the more vehemently you will want to dismiss this book.

In this age of computers and space shuttles, trusting love becomes a mystical act. Love cannot be proven. The part of your mind that seeks reasons, explanations and documentation will not be satisfied here. That doubting part of your mind will continue to doubt, you can count on it!

And why not? Doubt is the purpose of the doubting part of your mind. In fact, I invite you to indulge in doubt throughout this book. Giving yourself permission to doubt can do more to release doubt and rekindle faith than the struggle to suppress your skepticism will do.

But there is more to you than doubt. There is a part of you that yearns to trust and love again, and it is to this that I speak. This is not your mind, it is your heart, and the yearnings of the heart are frequently imprisoned by the reasonings of the mind. You need inspirations that by-pass the logical limitations of the mind to awaken and fuel these valid yearnings.

Love is mind-boggling. But the mind must be boggled when considering things that are none of its business. Love is the knowledge of the heart, the collective wisdom of the ages that resides deep within each of us. Love is the door to intuition, telepathy and profound spiritual experience. Yes, love *is* a mystical act, completely irrational, but without love to temper the rational, can we be certain of our survival, let along progress and evolution?

Most people are walking cases of suppressed joy and aliveness. At what point does the price of suppression become the cost of surgery? Freud said that you have to suppress to function. This attitude is based on a fundamental distrust of who we are. At what point is the cost no longer worth the pain?

Chapter III

Open mind,

Open heart

It may be that the world as we see it is largely an illusion, a funny house, a concoction of our own personal and worldview, a clever projection of associations from the past that camouflage what's really going on out there.

The mind thrives on familiarity. It loves to make sense of things, usually by fitting unknown phenomena into known mental categories. For example, you know what a home is because of all the houses called "home" you have experienced. Then, one day, you are exploring an archaeological site in Mexico. You come to a structure labelled "peasant home" and your mind immediately and compulsively looks for the familiar—a sleeping space, a cooking space, a john. You can only understand what you can relate to the past. Perhaps in your haste to make sense of things you project a bedroom onto a storage area or a kitchen onto a prayer room, but your mind leaves the site thinking it *knows*, with it's vision of reality intact.

In matters of the heart, it is difficult to experience love if you are "seeing" through the eyes of your past. For example: Your lover, normally articulate and witty at the dinner table, comes home on your birthday and opens the newspaper at the dinner table. You launch into a tirade about bad manners, rudeness and neglect and storm out of the house. Your lover, stunned, sits there thinking "I was only looking for a place we could go to celebrate."

What happened? Your father, it turns out, always hid behind *The Wall Street Journal* at the dinner table, creating a silent wall of upset between him and the rest of the family. The sight of your lover reading the paper triggers all the frustration and resentment of your childhood. In your mind, at that moment, your lover is your father. When you storm out of the room, your childhood is "running" you. You are not yourself. You are not in present time.

This is the law of projection. We are constantly projecting past incomplete feelings onto present reality. If love is blind, projection is what most clouds our vision. When we release the past from our minds and bodies, we connect with a deeper reality both inside and out. This deeper reality can be experienced by contemplating a flower, a cloud or the sea. Or from meditating with a mantra, yantra or tantra. When we ground ourselves in the reality of what is there and what is not, we witness the spiritual sub-strata behind the veil of physical illusion—the connective fabric of life itself. Thus the poet Blake could see the universe in a grain of sand long before scientists invented an atomic theory to describe the parallels between microscopic and cosmic formations. It is a mark of the insanity of Western culture that this spiritual vision is usually regarded as an altered state. The fact is, the illusions we project onto and mistake for reality comprise the altered state. We have our wires crossed!

The mind distorts reality by manifesting spirit into matter through false mental forms. The world of illusion that results is a source of much of our craziness!

An open mind is the key to an open heart!

If your mind is closed, so is your heart. The purpose of your mind is thinking, and the more you are able to notice your thoughts, the more aware (or conscious) you are. The more you know that the thoughts you most firmly believe become results in the physical universe, the more enlightened you are. But, if your mind is closed, the door to consciousness and enlightenment is locked and you will automatically project your unconsicous beliefs onto the world as though they were facts of life, fixed and unchangeable.

It is common knowledge now that a positive attitude is a great asset in life. Many athletes work on building a winning attitude as hard as they do on building their bodies. Muhammed Ali is a wonderful example. "I am the greatest!" he proclaimed to himself and the world, and he repeated this thought so often and with so much conviction that it became an agreed-upon "truth."

Confidence is having faith in something, and what you have faith in is instantly empowered!

How the Mind Works

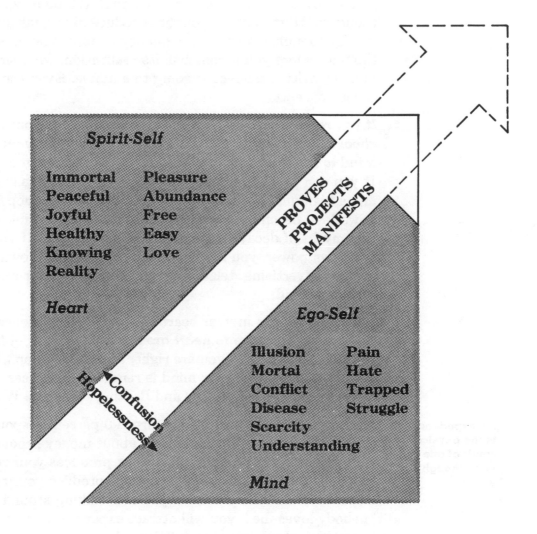

The thoughts you dwell on are the results you get: You always hit your mark. You can choose whether to project the illusions of the ego or the realities of the spirit into your life and the world. Of course, most thoughts are subconscious, so your results are always reflections of your subsconscious mind.

That is why self-confidence is so important. It empowers you to be the chief creative force in your life. And the way you create, whether you are conscious of it or not, is through the quality of your thoughts. High-quality thoughts produce high-quality results. Low-quality thoughts produce low-quality results. You must think a thought before you accomplish its realization, whether it's building a table or writing a novel or going to a movie. Even the origin of life is called conception!

☆ *If you rebel from this level of responsibility for your life, if you choose to "flow with it," you are simply inviting your subconscious mind to run your life, to manifest automatically your past beliefs.* If you don't reclaim your inherent power to believe in life and love and a high-quality existence, you render yourself hopeless and powerless, becoming a professional victim susceptible to the collective myths of decay, depression and destruction. If you don't "own" your own power, you invite those who know their own creative power—advertising, television and newspapers, for example—to control your mind.

What you believe in your heart is what you experience in your life. *The beliefs you take to heart are the results you get in life!* (And if you don't believe me, you are right, too!) If you don't believe in the power of your mind, your mind is rendered powerless and becomes a limbo for unrealized dreams and floating fantasies. What a waste!

An experience is the physical result of one or more thoughts.

Make no mistake about it—you are 100 percent responsible for every aspect of your life! Your thoughts about money produce your results with money; your thoughts about sex produces your results with sex; your thoughts about relationships produce your results with relationships. In other words, if you are walking around thinking, "nobody loves me," you will attract experiences to confirm your belief. In fact, *an experience is just the physical result of a thought.* And if you should attract someone who does love you, you will reject him or avoid him or think he is lying.

★ Everyone is always right, because everyone is always manifesting what he or she believes to be true. If you believe life is tough, you are right. You will collect all the evidence you need to convince yourself, if not others, what a struggle life is. If you believe life is easy, you are equally right. You will collect all the proof you need to feel how easy life is. This explains why totally contradictory belief systems can be equally documented. Questions of right and wrong become absurd issues once you realize that everyone is right in their own mind.

Your thoughts are more than just conclusions you draw from life; they are the prime causative factors of your experience. The more firmly the thought is rooted in your subconscious mind (which is a function of how often you've repeated the thought) the more "real" it seems to you. Of course, life is a struggle. Of course, life is easy. Of course, nobody loves me. Of course, everyone loves me. In a sense your life is a self-fulfilling prophecy, a secret subconscious scenario that you project onto life and take for life itself.

If you have been a professional victim all your life and suddenly understand that you created the whole thing, there is a temptation to stop blaming others and start blaming yourself. This is not the point. We are not talking about moral responsibility so much as physical and metaphysical responsibility. To say you are the cause of your life (not your parents or your country or the economy) is simply to state a law of nature as valid as the law of gravity. To take this information and make moral judgments with it is using your mind to punish yourself for your personal power. The fact is, you *are* responsible, but responsible does not mean guilty. You are innocent. If you have done "bad" things in your life, it was a result of "bad" thinking. Don't judge yourself for such errors; simply learn the lessons quickly. Let your results in life be your teachers. Become an enlightened detective, figuring out what subconscious thoughts are producing undesirable results in your life. Then change these thoughts. *Implant thoughts from your spirit-self and let go of thoughts from your ego-self* (see page 17). *This system of thought implanting, sometimes called affirmations, is a powerful and practical tool for changing your experience of love and life.*

Write down all your negative thoughts about (1) love, (2) life, (3) your body, (4) relationships and (5) money. Just free-associate, and fill up as many pages as necessary. When you feel you have really unloaded your mind, crumple up the pages and throw them away. Understand that these negatives are garbage and can be tossed away. This by-pass may not release all your negatives; it will, however, give you a sense that letting go is possible and that you are beginning to take charge of your life.

About this time, you are probably thinking, "Oh no, not another positive thinker!" You have my sympathies, rest assured. I am equally appalled by most simple-minded philosophies based on positive thinking. Most positive-thinking philosophies are based on the idea that you paint over all your negative conditioning with positive thoughts and, lo and behold, all your problems will disappear. This kind of philosophy is responsible for people who walk around smiling all the time, but when you're near them you cringe. The reason you cringe is that you sense there is garbage beneath the smile—garbage that has not been acknowledged, must less dumped. Traditional positive thinking is like putting a positive icing on a negative cake. It might taste good at first bite, but the aftertaste is awful.

Open heart therapy is based, not on positive thinking, but on attitudinal change. Since attitudes quickly become experiential truths, it is necessary to de-program the subconscious mind of the negative attitudes to which it tenaciously clings. **The system of thought implanting** allows you to plant positive ideas in the garden that is your subconscious mind and to weed out the negative ones. If you are a scrupulous gardener, you can uproot those old weeds and have a fruitful garden and a flourishing life.

The most powerful way to implant thoughts is through repetition. (After all, you planted your negative thoughts through repetition in the first place.) After you write an implant, draw a verticle line down the middle of the page. Write the implant over and over on the lefthand side of the page, about twenty times a day. On the right-hand side of the page is your response column. Every time you write the implant, take a breath and write your first reaction to it. These resisting thoughts are the weeds of your subconscious mind, weeds that can be eliminated by noticing them, feeling your feelings, and then returning to the positive attitude you wish to root in its place.

Implants for an Open Heart

Some positive attitudes you may want to start implanting are:

I love myself no matter what!

My body is a safe, comfortable and pleasurable place to be.

I deserve relationships that are fun, easy and supportive.

I am enough, I have enough, I do enough.

I now reclaim all my personal power.

I have everything I need to get everything I want.

Attitudinal Change: A Two-Way Process

Implant: New thought	Weed: Old thought
I am loved	Bullshit
I am loved	By whom?
I am loved	Not enough
I am loved	Then why do people disappoint me?
I am loved	I was as a child
I am loved	It's a struggle to get it
I am loved	I wish it were true
I am loved	Then why am I separate?
I am loved	Sadness
I am loved	Sore shoulders
I am loved	By some people
I am loved	I don't trust people
I am loved	I don't trust myself
I am loved	I don't trust love
I am loved	Sleepy
I am loved	A lot of people do care
I am loved	Maybe
I am loved	It feels good
I am loved	Yes
I am loved	God knows it's true

Focus on the positive. Notice but don't dwell on the response column. Remember, whatever comes up is on the way out and breathe consciously as you write the implant.

Chapter IV

More
mind stuff
to confuse you

If all this mind stuff is beginning to confuse you, relax and know it's working. If you turn back to the diagram of the mind (see page 17) you will notice "confusion" rests between your spirit-self and ego-self. The reason for this is that confusion represents a kind of middle ground, a state where your old belief system and your new attitudes have equal weight. Confusion means your old mind is loosening its grip and your new mind is taking root. So don't be dismayed **and don't struggle with confusion.** Struggle will return you to the ego. Just *be with* **confusion. Accept it as a state of contradiction. And continue to focus on your new implants.**

Sometimes you have to fall apart in order to find out how together you really are.

The same can be said of hopelessness. Although things seem dark when you're hopeless, the darkness is a new dawn in disguise. Hopelessness means you are losing hope, and hope is the opiate of the ego-self. **As long as you're stuck in hope, you still think some magical power outside yourself might correct a condition.** When you begin to lose that hope, you have begun the journey towards faith and certainty, aspects of your spirit-self. So when things look bleak, don't despair. Be willing to see that the way things look and the way they really are can be entirely different. Let the feeling be and breathe it out. Be patient. **Patience always outlasts hopelessness.** And remember, the darkest hour is just before the dawn.

Patience always outlasts hopelessness.

Your spirit-self is the true voice of your heart, your divine intuition, the guiding intelligence you can trust when your defenses are down and you are grounded in the moment. Your spirit-self is the reality you mistake for the dream—as a child you were taught to dismiss this part of yourself, to discount your visions and intuition. You became socially well-adjusted, but what a price you paid!

Your ego-self is the voice of your mind, the voice of reason, the calculating, scheming part of you. Your ego is not bad. It developed to protect you and insure your survival in a world you did not understand. As such, your ego, as well as your spirit, is based on love.

Your spirit-self is the truth you've learned not to believe in. Your ego-self is the lie you've learned to trust. Spiritual people are often called dreamers by ego people. The truth is, the ego-self is the dream taken for reality. (Our obsession with horror films is based on the drive to wake up safely from the nightmare. Horror films are an excellent opportunity to lessen fear of the unknown. There is nothing so terrible within or without us that we cannot outlast by screaming and crying and breathing deeply. Indeed, what we most fear is the joy and aliveness suppressed beneath the fear and numbness.) Letting go of the illusion represents a death to the ego, and the ego will tempt you back into itself.

It is important to remember that you are the dreamer as well as the dreamed. If you load your arrows (see page 22) with ego thoughts, you are the hunter, fighting to survive in a world you do not trust. If you, on the other hand, load your arrows with spiritual inspirations, you are a spiritual warrior and a force to be reckoned with on the planet.

Your strength is stronger than your weakness.

If an open mind is the key to an open heart, high-quality thinking is the door to high-quality living. By "high-quality" I mean, quite simply, thoughts that generate love, that all-pervasive sense of well-being, for yourself and others. The most enlightened thoughts are the most loving ones. You can become a force of love in the world if you dwell in the realm of loving thoughts and observe others without matching their energy. When your ego tries to tempt you with negativity, remember that your thoughts are just thoughts, and can easily be released by focusing your mind on implants from your spirit-self and letting go of the energy it takes to hold onto old ideas.

The more you focus on love, the more love will expand in your life. Take the high-quality thought "The world is a safe and wonderful place to be!" The more you dwell on this thought, the more you notice people enjoying their lives, and the more they share their joy, the more of an epidemic it becomes. To be sure, we must not ignore the negative—the poor, the hungry, the imprisoned—or the problems we face will grow more powerful. We must notice these problems and dwell with more conviction on the ideals we seek to manifest. The important thing is to throw your weight behind the love, not the hate, in the world.

You must be willing to go out there and make a difference with your dreams, participating in life 100 percent, which I will discuss later. For now, know this: Until you choose to play the game of life fully, all your enlightenment and all your idealism are a mind game created by your ego to amuse you while you avoid life completely. You cannot hide in a closet all day and night, writing high-quality thoughts a million times, and hope to open the door to heaven-on-earth in the morning. Most of us have not yet attained that level of mastery!

If your mind is closed, your ego has a strangle-hold on your life. You probably think hundreds of thousands of thoughts every day, most of which are unconscious. Many of these thoughts are repeated each day: "Time to wake up!," "Gotta go to work!," "Gotta catch the train!" These surface thoughts are automatic commands you've programmed yourself to obey, although you probably wish you didn't have to. This level of thinking is usually based on struggle, pain and the need to earn approval in order to survive.

Beneath this level of thinking is the level of helplessness—thoughts like "I can't get up," "I can't get the job done," "I can't make the train." Moving to a still deeper level, you reach thoughts based on resentment and revenge, such as "I don't want to get up," "I don't want to go to work," "I don't want to catch the damn train!"

Write the following statement at the top of a piece of paper and complete it. "If I knew I made a difference, something I'd be doing that I'm not doing now in my life is . . ." Write down as many things as you can think of. Are you willing to schedule these things into your calendar?

Still further down in your subconscious is the level of *birth trauma*, producing thoughts like "It hurts too much to try." Now you're reaching some basic beliefs about yourself and life. Thoughts like "It's not worth the effort," "I don't deserve to live," "I'm bad," "There's something wrong with me," "My love hurts people," or "I'll never make it." This is the level of Primal Law, your most negative dominant consciousness factor! This all-powerful thought, usually a conclusion you made at birth, about yourself and life is a generalization you have always believed and never released. Your Primal Law is so basic to your personality that it seems more like a fact of life than a mere thought. Your Primal Law is something you carry in every cell of your body; it is the very "eyes" through which you see life. Your Primal Law can be difficult to locate because your ego does not want to be dismantled at the core.

Primal laws are powerful feelings that we strongly defend and only reluctantly release. If you think "I have to struggle to survive" because you struggled through the birth canal to make it in the first place, you will not easily relinquish the thought even if you see that believing it is causing more struggle in your life. This is a totally reasonable position when you stop to consider that, first, you've held this thought so deeply it's become embodied on a cellular level, and, second, it's a life-and-death matter. If, in your mind, struggle is a necessity of life, and if, in your body, the cells have been programmed with this thought, you'd be foolish to change your mind before you had sufficient proof that your body would survive. In other words *your body will resist new ideas until it feels safe with those ideas.*

Why struggle to earn the love you're already worth?

The ramifications of your Primal Law are monumental. If you believe you have to struggle to survive, you will struggle at work, play, relationships, health, whatever. If you believe that you can't trust anyone, another primal variation, you won't trust your friends, boss, co-workers, lovers, children or parents. Since your entire personality is formed in reaction to such thoughts, dismantling these primal belief systems is a tricky business, and even recognizing them can take some detective work. For example, if you believe you always hurt the one you love because you thought you caused your mother pain at birth, you might have formed a reactive lifestyle.

Levels of the Mind

Thought	*Origin*
"I have to do that!"	Struggle to survive, approval
"I can't do that!"	Helplessness
"I don't want to do it!"	Resentment
"You can't make me do it!"	Revenge
"It hurts too much to try!"	Birth
"I don't deserve to live!"	Guilt, Primal Law
"It's hopeless anyway!"	Death

Primal Law Chart

Primal Law	Behavior
"I can't make it."	Struggle, incompletion, intense drive to succeed, failure.
"My love hurts others."	Violent temper, strong need to help others (to compensate for guilt), nice guy or good girl act to protect those you love from yourself.
"Something's wrong with me."	Illness- or accident-prone; perfectionist syndrome.
"Nobody notices me."	Hides a lot, quiet, passive, or else a deep need to stand out, call attention to oneself, star syndrome.
"I'm misunderstood."	Unclear communication, overly verbal, not satisfied with responses, overly concerned with other people's reactions.
"I'm ugly."	Either disheveled in appearance or else vain, trying to hide behind false beauty; perhaps artistic (to create a substitute beauty.)
"I'm a disappointment" (if you felt unwanted or the wrong sex).	Under-achiever, or else a strong need to make everyone happy to compensate for your fear of letting them down.
"I'm stupid."	Either a poor student or an intense need to understand and seem intelligent, but never really believing it.
"I don't want to be here" ("I'm unwanted").	Strong leaving pattern: moving a lot, leaving jobs or relationships.

Eternal Law

"I can survive relaxation."
"I've got it made."
"Taking it easy supports my success."

"I create the pain and pleasure in my life, and others do it in their lives."
"My love is good enough for me and everyone else."
"My love is a healing force in the world."

"I'm perfect just the way I am."

"I acknowledge my divine essence and so does everyone else."

"I express myself fully and clearly."
"What I say always hits its target."

"I am a beautiful, lovable person, attractive to myself and others."

"I am a wonderful surprise."
"I am God's gift to the world and the world is God's gift to me."

"My connection to infinite intelligence is unlimited."
"I'm smarter than I think."

"I am always at the perfect place at the perfect time."
"It's safe to stay."
"I belong."

You might be super-nice, gentle and self-effacing. Perhaps you're a teacher, social worker or doctor, someone whose life is dedicated to helping others. If your greatest fear is hurting people, it's logical you'd try to help instead, both to release your primal guilt and to prove to yourself and the world that you are, after all, a good person. But somewhere in your life, probably with the person you're closest to, your Primal Law will erupt, rekindling that you do, in fact, hurt the ones you love. Maybe you'll find yourself divorced, alone and buried in your work of helping people.

If your Primal Law is "Nobody notices me," because you were left alone for a long time in the nursery after your birth, you might become an actor, model or topless dancer to gain the attention you crave (see Primal Law chart, page 30).

Sometimes people think that if they give up allegiance to their law, they will lose their motivation to work and their survival will be threatened. This is just the ego-self speaking, trying to convince you that you have to justify your existence because you are guilty. Once you see the ego in its full blaze of glory, you can begin to laugh at all its dirty tricks. Converting your Primal Law to your Eternal Law, the simple positive version of the thought, does not mean you lose motivation. On the contrary, you will be motivated to help others and share love out of your natural goodness, rather than a need to work off your guilt.

Getting on the right side of your law causes a quantum shift in the quality of your life! The way to get on the right side of the Law is, first of all, to acknowledge you're on the wrong side and that it's safe to change your mind. Don't defend your struggle and secretly wish life were easier. Admit to yourself (and others) how attached you are to your Law. Acknowledging is a choice towards consciousness and away from ignorance. To know your own mind is to understand your whole life!

Discover your Primal Law! Make a list of your five most negative thoughts about yourself. Notice how your mind tries to avoid this by-pass. You might be thinking "I can't do this," not realizing that "I can't do it" is your Primal Law. Or maybe you discard three of the five and are left with your two most fundamental thoughts. Your mind says "I can't make up my mind!" That's it. Your law, which keeps you indecisive all your life. Circle your Primal Law, that omnipresent thought you don't want to see, that bubble within which you move through life. Once you've found it, let yourself feel it. Sinking into the apparent reality of your Primal Law is an important phase in releasing it. Let yourself experience the energy in your body around this thought. Walk around for a day consciously looking at life through your Law. Just observe how life works in response to it. Remember to breath deeply. When you feel you have completed this part of the by-pass, go on to the next part. Create your Eternal Law, the simple positive variation of your Primal Law. For example, if your Primal Law is "There's something wrong with me," your Eternal Law should be something like "I'm perfect just the way I am!" If your Primal Law is "I always hurt the ones I love," your Eternal Law might be "My love is a healing force in all my relationships." Check the Primal Law chart on page 30 for suggestions. Now begin to work consciously with your Eternal Law. Write it twenty times a day with a response column, to weed out subconscious opposition to embodying this thought fully. Walk around viewing life through your new thought. See what a difference it makes.

Admit that you've repeated your Primal Law so many times in thought, word and deed that it seems more like natural law than personal addiction. Indeed, if you feel struggle is necessary, you will habitually attract and witness struggle in the world. Your mind is like a magnet and always attracts the facts it needs in order to hold onto itself.

After acknowledging your allegiance to the law, feel your desire to change your life and let that desire become a commitment to legislate a new law, an Eternal Law. You must have a deep desire in your heart to transform your ground of being in order to bring about a change in your experience.

You must change your mind if your life is to change! That is why it is so important to keep an open mind. It gives you the power to be creative. To get on the right side of the law, conceive of being there.

Learn to believe in a new reality. Affirm with your heart "I can survive, whether I struggle or not," "I have the right to exist," "It's safe to take it easy," "My love is good enough for me and everyone else." Plant your Eternal Law in the garden that is your subconscious mind, and repeat such thoughts until they take root in the core of your being. Meanwhile, weed out all opposing thoughts.

If you take care of your mind, your mind will take care of you. Once you open the door, your mind will answer the questions you ask it. Be a clever detective and practice interrogating your own mind as though it were a key witness. This self-interrogation process is extremely valuable in uprooting negative consciousness factors. If you have a problem in your life, say you're a woman and the men you love always seem to leave you, take responsibility for creating the problem. Even though your ego-self wants to keep you a victim, your spirit-self now knows it creates everything. If there's an undesirable situation in your life, one you consciously did not choose, admit that you must have a strong subconscious belief affecting the matter. It is then time for self-interrogation. Write on a piece of paper "The reason I create men leaving me is . . ." and list all the thoughts you have on the subject. When you find the bottom-line thoughts, your body will react in an unmistakable manner. Maybe it's simply your Primal Law that's driving men away. Maybe you never finished mourning your father, who died when you were ten. When you locate the one or two most basic causes, turn them into positive thoughts and implant them in your subconscious mind through repetition. If it's a matter of mourning, work with a thought like "I now release my father forever," and breathe deeply through the feelings that surface. Self-interrogation is a valuable aspect of self-cleansing.

If you take responsibility, without guilt, for the creations of your life and clear out your negative beliefs, you will produce a quantum attitudinal transformation in your life and you will naturally manifest the true desires of your spirit-self, which comprise your true purpose in life.

Identity Chart

Who You Pretend to Be	Self-image	Mr. Niceguy, Ms. Goodgirl
Who You Fear You Are	Primal Law	A bad person
Who You Really Are	Eternal Law	Innocent, good and loving

The chart helps to explain how we fluctuate through life, pretending to be good, but afraid people will discover our inherent badness. Most people go through life carefully selecting which parts of themselves to reveal. If you want someone to like you, you show them what you think are your most likeable traits. This seems to make sense, but immediately traps you. The parts of yourself you hide from those you love become walls around your heart, and you cannot surrender to love completely if part of you is busy protecting your hidden self. I always recommend that people do what my wife Mallie and I did when we met: Put your worst foot forward first. Let your partner see all the "horrible" things about yourself. Then you'll never have to hide in your relationship; moreover, you'll know your partner really loves you if he or she can accept these traits. Also, you'll quickly see that your fears about who you are and your compensating Niceguy or Goodgirl act are really unnecessary—that you are, in fact, a good person with loving intentions.

Family means loving each other even when there's a difference of opinion.

As you become more conscious of the quality of your thoughts, as you open your mind to higher possibilities, remember to respect others wherever they are on their path through life. One of the secrets to keeping your heart open is to honor your own belief system while loving others whether or not their ideas agree with yours. Even in the best of families there can be a healthy difference of opinion. In fact, conflicting thoughts need not be a ground for war; they can be an opportunity to evolve yet higher ideas which are mutually beneficial to more people.

Any belief system, no matter how enlightened, becomes a trap when it becomes an excuse for closing your heart to others. Compassion for your fellow men and women must be a higher priority than your judgments in order to keep love flowing in your life. We all have our ideas. The mind is constantly evaluating, judging and comparing. Once you're secure in your point of view, you can move to a higher lever in which you recognize that your opinions are just opinions and don't let them interfere with your love for yourself and others. You have a right to your opinions, and everyone else has a right to theirs!

Let your ethics be grounded on the priority of love. Let love be the rock on which you build your ethics. Sometimes I tell my students "I'd rather win love than arguments." By this I mean that, when I find myself in the midst of a difference of opinion, giving up my investment in being right and surrendering to love is often practical and productive.

When I first met my wife, we quickly realized that we both loved to be right. This attachment to our particular beliefs had led to considerable conflict in our previous relationships and we knew we didn't want to repeat that pattern. So we created a game, The Right Day Game, which we have since shared with thousands. In this game one person gets to be "right" for a day or a week, while the partner gets to agree. No matter what the "right" person says—even, "Look, it's snowing," on a hot August day—the partner must agree. "Hey, you're right. Let's build a snowman." This game makes the whole issue of right and wrong a joke, and it gives you an opportunity to see how brilliant your partner is. I recommend you try this process, switching frequently, until the whole issue loses its emotional charge. The major thing to remember is that love is more valuable than war, and whether the battlefield is in your mind, in your relationships or between two countries, the peace-making mission begins within yourself. Only when you have given up the fight within will you be able to be a peace generator.

I'd rather win love than arguments!

If you have a passion for peace, you are a force to be reckoned with on the planet.

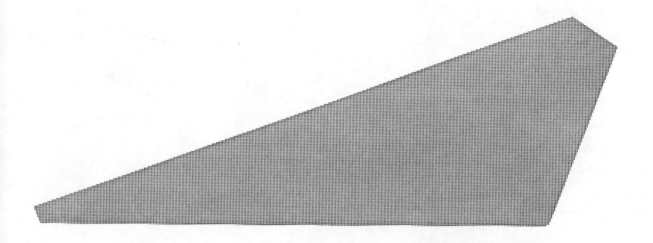

Chapter V

Can't feel, Can't Heal

Most people I meet suffer from a fair amount of "emotional anesthesia." They have suppressed their feelings so regularly for so long that they hardly even know what they feel any more. Whenever an intense feeling begins to emerge, they hold their breath, literally pushing carbon dioxide back into their bloodstream and the cells of their bodies, causing a major "numbing out" of the five senses. Much of what we take to be signs of aging is, in my opinion, the cumulative effect of years of emotional anesthesia.

What you can't feel, you can't heal.

Feelings are energy moving through your body with specific thoughts propelling them, usually memories of incomplete experiences. For example, your lover is going away on a business trip. Your body swells up with a warm, loving energy, but subconsciously remembering your father's death when you were a child, a death that occurred while he was away on business, you begin to feel the pain you never released, and the love gets confused with the loss in your mind. You therefore call the feeling "sadness."

You are about to get on a roller coaster. A friend turns to you and says "God, this is exciting!" You look into your body and the aliveness you feel is uncontrollable. But remembering a time you went horseback riding and felt similar sensations, only to fall off the horse and break your leg, you are now cautious. You have learned to call your excitement "fear."

Every feeling is a feeling of aliveness and, if not suppressed, will lead to greater love.

Feelings are relative to the feel-er. One man's anger is another man's terror. It depends on your associations with (1) the activating stimuli and (2) the particular energy form you feel in your body.

One thing certain about feelings is that the energy at their core is a healing force and, if not suppressed, will lead to an all-pervasive sense of well-being: love. Anyone who's had a good cry or scream and come out on the other side can testify to this.

All your feelings are valid! As children we often get punished for our feelings. Our parents will do anything to shut us up. A baby cries; a mother stuffs a bottle in its mouth. A six-year-old boy screams at his father; he is sent to his room without dinner. In most families there is an acceptable code of emotional repression, depending on the comfort level of the parents. We learn very early that expressing feelings can be risky business that leads to separation from those we love. So we are programmed to control ourselves, which often means stuffing our feelings back into the cells of our bodies, an unhealthy act that causes more tension, frustration and pain in the body. Feelings need to come out if we are to be whole again. The dilemma of feelings is how to get through them—or how to let them get through us.

Love is the master cleanser. Love wants to flush out all your pain and misery and make you feel whole again. The more you are loved, however, the more all your feelings emerge. *Love activates you for the purpose of healing you, but the less you trust love the more tenaciously you will cling to your resistance.* The love will feel like quicksand, and your ego like a helping hand.

And so it goes. You keep attracting the love you need to heal yourself, but when your ass is on the line you choose to retreat rather than risk total surrender. The pain you feel is the result of the effort it takes to hold onto your ego when your spirit is screaming "Let go, you fool!"

Every upset is a set-up! You subconsciously set up a situation to activate all your suppressed and unresolved feelings, but when the feelings come up you don't have the safety or support to go through them. So you push them back down until the next time. Often, you blame your partner for your lack of courage. You withhold asking for what you want, withdraw your love, and then resent your partner for not reading your mind. This **withhold, withdraw, resent** syndrome is extremely subtle and dangerous to relationships. The solution is simply to be direct in your communication. People who don't ask for what they want have little right to complain about not getting it.

Find a friend who loves you, preferably someone reading this book. This is a two-person by-pass. Sit opposite each other. Decide who will "give" and who will "receive" first. After three minutes, switch roles. The giver repeats the following statement over and over to the receiver, who does nothing except breathe and notice his thoughts and body sensations: "I love you and will never leave you!" Really pay attention to how uncomfortable it can be to hear the words your heart most wants to believe. Breathe out the discomfort. Be at ease with greater amounts of love!

To feel is to be vulnerable, and to be vulnerable is to be out of control. Most of us dread being out of control. Almost everything you do in life is based on your need to control, for fear that if you let go someone else will control you. You want to control friends, family, lovers, money and feelings. Control is the way the ego plays God. Control is why most people prefer giving love to receiving love, much as they deny it. As long as you are the one giving, you are in the driver's seat. You can turn, slow down or stop any time you want. But if someone is directing a lot of love your way, fear will come up very quickly; you'll feel yourself sliding into the quicksand.

Whatever comes up is on the way out.

The more you receive love, the more you feel. If you know that whatever comes up is on its way out, if you've established safety in your relationships by telling the truth and seeing you are accepted as you are, if you feel supported—then and only then will you surrender and complete the healing process.

Many old-fashioned men and modern women hide behind a macho act. They hold themselves together at any cost, not allowing anything or anyone to touch them deeply. Inside they tend to feel weak and helpless, but they don't have the inner safety to show themselves. They study karate, kung fu, body building—so they have the power to kill, but not the strength to feel.

What does it mean to be "together?" Certainly not to hold yourself together for fear that if you let go you'd disintegrate. That's not strength, that's paralysis—a rigid, brittle stance toward life. To be whole means you can fall apart once in a while and pick up the pieces again. *You must let go into your feelings in order to grow.* And you must contract and integrate sometimes too.

Expansion and contraction are two aspects of one universal force. The heart beats, protoplasm pulsates, stars twinkle—all of life is breathing in and out, vibrating, expanding and contracting. People get in trouble when they're going through a natural period of contraction, but wishing they were expanding, or vice versa. This is the ego's need to resist the tide of life. Why waste your energy resisting the direction your life is naturally moving? Resistance creates tension, conflict and pain, while surrender leads to peace, ease and satisfaction. Happiness results from choosing to let go of your projections and trust life to bring you and your purpose together. To grow is to discover your own internal rhythm of opening and closing and to honor that highly personal process.

Intimacy means "into-me-see"!

But first you must be willing to open. Intimacy is the result of revealing yourself to others, a frightening proposition to most of us. **Intimacy means "into-me-see."** The more I let you see into me, the more intimate I tend to feel with you. But if I'm too scared to be vulnerable, thinking you'll see who I fear I am (namely, my Primal Law), then I'll withdraw, disconnect and separate myself from you, never surrendering to my real hidden self.

The conflict between our addiction to privacy and our longing for intimacy runs our lives! Most of us have developed extremely sophisticated defense systems behind which we hide. We are master hiders; we put the Pentagon to shame with our secret data! We carefully select which aspects of ourselves to reveal, hiding what we dislike so nobody will notice and disapprove. The game we play goes like this: I'll seduce you with my most lovable qualities, but I won't really let you into my heart, because if you ever saw who I really am you'd reject me.

Intimacy is a process of self-discovery. It requires courage, but the rewards are enormous. You find out how safe you are with your feelings; you find out how lovable you are even when vulnerable; you discover the joy of being touched deeply. The fear you feel when you are drawn towards greater intimacy is a healthy fear, not a danger sign.

Fear is an invitation to greater safety with more energy.

Fear is frequently an invitation to *greater safety with more energy.* You are about to get on that roller coaster again. The memory of falling off the horse flashes before your eyes. You take a chance. You board the ride. You have a terrific time. Your fear was just the prelude to more fun than you were used to. Love can be a roller coaster too, and it can have more loops than Lightning loops and steeper drops than the Cyclone. Your fear of the ride is not a problem—it is more the attraction that gets you to the ticket window. The more we take risks, the more our trepidations turn into peak experiences!

★ So fear can become our friend, an exciting energy affording us an opportunity to release more old hurt. *"Fear forward," a friend once told us.* Columbus discovered America. Astronauts step on the moon. Lovers seek new levels of surrender. There are no limits to how far the heart can go.

Anger is a tricky emotion, probably the least socially acceptable feeling. *Anger is a lot of energy propelled by the thought of attack.* When you are not safe with your hurt and fear (which usually lie beneath anger), when your vulnerability activates the thought that people are out to get you, you retaliate. Anger is the survival emotion; in your mind, it's "kill or be killed."

The worst thing about anger is that, of all the emotions, it seems to cause the most separation in our loving relationships. This is probably because our parents were so uncomfortable with their angry feelings and therefore disapproved of us whenever we exploded. Maybe they even hit us.

If you cannot express your anger appropriately and without guilt (i.e., thinking it hurts people), you will suppress it every time you feel it and it will build into major resentments. The resentment will numb your heart to the point where you feel ice cold towards those you really love.

☆ *The key to handling present-time anger is always to share your hurt. The more you communicate your hurt to people the less you will need to get angry to protect yourself.*

There are also several games you can play to handle, first resentment, then anger. The *wet truth game* is one we invented to prevent the accumulation of resentment. You get in the bathtub each night with your mate. Each of you gets an equal amount of time to communicate frustrations from the day—thoughts like "I hated you when you didn't screw the toothpaste cap back on," "I'm jealous of your sister," "I wanted to leave you when you kept me waiting a half an hour at lunch." Thoughts like these are usually withheld in most relationships. Trivial though they seem, if not communicated they can become major blocks to feeling the flow of love. If you are on the receiving end of this process, your job is to breathe, say "thank you" after each communication, laugh when you can, and, under no circumstances, attempt to defend yourself. See these thoughts as on the way out. Don't add energy to what is being discharged. Remember that you are innocent, and peace needs no defense. When each of you has taken a turn, hug each other, get out of the tub, and let the water flow down the drain. You are cleansed and ready for bed.

Innocence can neither be created nor destroyed.

Another game you can play with anger we call the *creative blame* game. This is best done with an enlightened friend or therapist. In this game the therapist is a surrogate who plays the part of someone you love but resent and are willing to forgive. You kneel opposite each other, about three feet apart. Both breathe deeply. No physical contact is allowed. (Pounding pillows or fighting with batakas can be valuable.) When you are ready, without rehearsing, you blast the surrogate with all the angry energy and thoughts you've been holding. ("I hated you when you divorced Dad," "I can't stand your martyr act!") Keep blasting until you go beyond the point of exhaustion and feel enlivened. (Actually the point of exhaustion is your ego trying to seduce you into futility, so don't give up!) Continue until you feel complete, remembering to breathe at all times and keep your eyes open all the way. When you are finished, just lie down and keep breathing, relaxing until you feel grounded.

If you are on the receiving end of the creative blame game, it is important to let the energy pass through you and remind yourself you are not the object of the blame. Also, maintain eye contact with your partner and look for the love that is driving the anger out. Don't allow your partner to withdraw into sadness, sorrow or self-pity (socially acceptable cop-outs). Remember, a true healer is someone who does not match energy, who gives someone space in which to heal himself (self-healing is the only real healing), and who acknowledges releases when they occur without judging resistance when it blocks the way.

Another simple technique that can accelerate the release of anger is taking the energy, attaching a positive thought to it, and shouting in the shower or your car (windows shut, please) or the woods. What you don't want to do is dump your anger on other people. There are, as I have described, appropriate ways to release rage. You don't have to lambast someone, then get stuck in the guilt that confirms your Primal Law and feel sorry for yourself. Self-pity is the mind's victory; your ego gets to condescend to your spirit.

You don't have to suppress your anger ever again. You can assert yourself in life, ask for what you want, learn to take no for an answer and deal with old rage and hurt in appropriate ways. If you are suppressing anger you will know, because you will tend to attract angry people to you. They are actually your gurus, teaching you it is safe to be angry. Whenever you reject anger, or anything else for that matter, you recreate it in larger doses to emphasize the lesson. The universe is infinitely generous in the opportunities it gives you to be unconditionally loving of yourself and others. Your external relationships are always the perfect mirrors of your subconscious mind!

It is the same with sadness. If you get upset whenever someone is sad, if you have a compulsive need to leave or to comfort someone who is crying, take a breath and take a look at your own feelings. Give the other person room to move through his or her grief.

Perhaps it is you who are uncomfortable with your own suppressed tears. Perhaps your eyes itch because there is some loss you have not completed mourning. Never miss an opportunity to cry. A backlog of grief is harmful to the body. Many doctors now believe that suppressed grief and resentment can produce cancerous cells in the body.

The clear message here is to feel and express, but always appropriately. Don't dump on others or yourself! Sometimes people get stuck in self-expression, the drama of feelings, and cling to theatrics as a last-ditch effort to avoid a complete release. Expressing without breathing is not releasing. It is the breathing while you're feeling that moves and eventually grounds the energy. Your job, meanwhile, is to watch your thoughts go by without tackling any of them.

Most people have a distorted view of forgiveness. If you come to me and ask my forgiveness for something and I say "Okay, I forgive you," what am I really saying? My subtext is: Yes, you have really done me wrong, but out of the bigness of my heart I will condescend to forgive you. Obviously, this kind of forgiveness produces little healing and, in fact, can add resentment. You might walk away thinking "Who the hell is he to forgive me?"

Forgiveness is the master erase (see *A Course in Miracles*). If you are clinging to old resentment, your mind is selectively remembering only the negative impressions you have of someone. *To forgive is to choose consciously to remember only the positive impressions, to let go of all else, to selectively dwell in the realm of loving thoughts.* To resent, on the other hand is to remember only the negative impressions. If you remembered the good stuff, how could you stay angry so long?

If you've had an upset with someone, the first thing to do is acknowledge that you created it. No matter how much you are tempted to play the victim, you must take responsibility for something in your subconscious mind that attracted this situation for learning and healing purposes. It is necessary, before you can forgive someone else, to forgive yourself for this unpleasant creation. Also, forgive yourself for blaming the other person and reducing yourself to a helpless victim. Only then can you forgive the other person for his role in creating the upset. Make a conscious choice not to get even. You know this is the wise choice, since revenge will only cause you pain. You are now enlightened enough to see that there was no wrongdoing involved, only interlocking subconscious patterns. If your boyfriend left you, perhaps it was because your dad died when you were a child; your boyfriend's pattern might be from birth: "I've got to get out of here to survive!" There is no one to blame, only love, the master cleanser, wanting to purge you of old wounds. You both set up the separation to heal yourselves.

The only one you get even with is yourself.

Forgiveness is its own reward.

Forgiveness is its own reward! When you forgive someone, you receive the joy of opening your heart and feeling your love again. A wall melts. That all-pervasive warmth moves through your body again. Whether the other person forgives you is almost irrelevant, though he usually will, soon after you release your guilt by forgiving yourself.

Sondra Ray's "forgiveness diet" is a process that takes a month to do but is well worth the time and energy. You work with four forgiveness implants, each for a week. You write each statement seventy times a day for seven days. Begin by forgiving your father: "I forgive my father completely!" Then move on to your mother: "I forgive my mother completely!" Then move on to yourself: "I forgive myself completely!" And finally, forgive God: "I forgive God completely!" If one month is not enough, repeat this diet as often as necessary until you feel release in your life.

It is important to set your parents free. Forgive them completely. However badly you think they treated you, you know they did the best they could, given the circumstances of their lives. Many grown people hold onto their resentment towards their parents as an excuse for not doing what they want in life. They pretend that their parents still have some magical hold on them. Or they "fail" at life to show the world what a miserable job the parents did. Your parents did what they did. If they gave you money instead of love, perhaps it was because they grew up during the Depression and financial security became the most basic expression of love they knew. If they disapproved of you a lot, their intention was to support your growth, and they did it the way their parents did it with them. At worst your parents were unconscious victims of their own family tradition.

Make a list of 300 things you're grateful for: 100 things you have, 100 qualities you possess, and 100 things you've done in your life. You will be amazed at what a treasure chest your life is.

You are already in possession of life's most precious possession, which is life itself.

Where does the buck stop? It's time to stop waiting for them to set you free. Only you can give yourself that freedom. But you can set your parents free in your heart. Give them the acceptance and unconditional love you always wanted from them. Stop trying to change them, to save them. They've chosen their lives and they have as much right to their style of thinking and living as you do. If you can't practice "live and let live" with them, how will you ever practice it with your mate, your friends, your business associates? Your relationships will always be stuck, your heart will always be shut, to the extent that you have not forgiven your parents.

When forgiveness replaces resentment in your heart, you will find yourself feeling more and more grateful. Gratitude is, quite simply, being thankful for your life—for the love, the pleasure and the opportunities to grow. The more grateful you are, the more you will have to be grateful for! Don't live a life of sorrow, bitterness and regret. Focus your mind's eye on the richness of your life. You always have the choice. When a glass is half full of water, you can dwell on the fullness or the emptiness. What you focus on, expands!

Most "problems" in your life are emotional. Without an emotional charge a problem is a lesson or challenge—something to be welcomed, not dreaded.

Implants for a Healthy Emotional Life

General

All my feelings are valid!

I forgive myself for suppressing my feelings.

I forgive my parents for disapproving of my feelings.

I forgive my parents for suppressing their feelings.

I have the right to feel the way I do!

It's safe to feel my feelings!

I can feel and express my feelings
without undesirable consequences.

I can now express all my feelings easily and appropriately
and with good to all concerned!

Whenever I share my feelings, people see the love behind them.

I am a good person no matter what I feel!

Fear

It's safe to be scared!

Just because I'm afraid doesn't mean I'm in danger.

My body is a safe and pleasurable place to be.

I can have all the pleasure I want without painful consequences.

My future is safe and full of wonderful surprises.

Nobody wants to hurt me.

Whenever I feel afraid, I can relax, breathe
and get safe in my body again.

Anger

It's safe to get angry.

It's human to get angry.

Anger is harmless.

I always express my anger appropriately.

I forgive myself for all the times I
    expressed my anger inappropriately.

I forgive myself for thinking I was a victim!

I no longer need to separate myself when I'm angry.

People accept and love me even when I'm angry.

I can get what I want!

I can take no for an answer.

I'd rather win love than arguments.

Peace needs no defense.

Sadness

I set my father free.

I set my mother free.

I never lose anything of lasting value.

I never lose anything that's for my highest good.

Whenever I seem to lose, a bigger win is on its way.

It's safe to feel my sadness.

Crying is manly.

There is always joy beneath my sadness.

I can let go of my sadness without losing love.

I deserve to be happy!

Select a *"problem" you're willing to eliminate. Write it down as simply as possible. Now, do a self-interrogation. Write "The reason I created _____ is . . ." and start listing whatever associations your mind reveals. When you hit the real cause, you'll feel it in your body. Then do two things: (1) create a positive implant to affirm daily (with a response column) and (2) decide on an appropriate course of action in the physical universe and schedule it into your calendar.*

Every problem was once a solution to a previous problem!

For example, you're overweight. Once you were thin and vulnerable, perhaps at birth. Then you were hurt. Your parents were worried about you and you felt their concern. You concluded "It's not safe to be little!" and "My parents want me to be bigger." So you decided both to please your parents and to cushion yourself from anticipated hardships of life with fat cells. Your weight "problem" is actually a solution to your fear problem—a shelter from the storm.

Every problem was once a solution to a previous problem.

The way to solve a problem is, first, change the thought that caused the problem: "It is now safe and pleasurable to be little." Then, act appropriately in the physical universe—eat less and exercise. If you do the latter without doing the former, it won't work. No amount of struggle can overcome, for very long, a negative thought to which you are addicted. Whatever you do, don't use your problem to make yourself wrong and prove your Primal Law: "You see, I was right, there *is* something wrong with me: I'm fat!" Beating yourself up for a problem only adds mass to the problem, making its elimination more difficult.

Chapter VI

Birth,
an unforgettable experience

Whenever I tell people about my birth memories, many of them react with surprise. "It's impossible!" says one. "I can't even remember when I was ten," says another. "How can you be sure that's what really happened?" asks a third. Why should it be so amazing that the birth memory lies within each of us? After all, it is a singular experience, a uniquely powerful experience, more significant than your first day of school or your first kiss or the first time you made love—things most people can easily recall. That most people do not remember their births is a function, not so much of time, but of how incredibly intense it was, how much anesthesia was used, and the illusion that in order to remember it one would have to relive the pain.

As I have suggested, much of our ambivalence about love begins with birth, if not earlier. Recent studies in prenatal psychology conclude that even in the womb we are busy little creatures, receiving and deciphering information from the outside world, as well as expressing our reactions and opinions through a primitive body language (see Dr. Thomas Verny's book, *The Secret Life of the Unborn Child*).

In the beginning love flowed freely through your whole universe. You were conceived in a moment of love, and in the womb love grew into human beingness. Your mother's nourshing love accelerated your growth. You were a part of this mother-love, come from father-love.

The womb, it would seem, is a fairly pleasant journey for most of us. (Certainly we spend enough time creating substitute wombs in life.) Floating on a gentle sea of amniotic fluid, all your needs are provided for. (How many of us bring this same primal longing to our loving relationships?) Nourished and "breathed" through the umbilical cord, you have nothing to do but sleep and grow and learn. What an ideal learning situation it is too! Insulated from external turbulance, you are nonetheless telepathically open to messages from the universe, as well as intimately connected to your mother's nervous system and thereby to her brain. Recent learning experiments in sensory deprivation tanks as well as on sleeping subjects indicate that the womb would be the perfect place to educate oneself. Depending on how aware your parents were, you may have communicated regularly with them during pregnancy, recognizing the sounds of their voices as well as the emotional vibrations passing between them.

Gradually you grew bigger and bigger, and your once endless universe became cramped quarters. You began to thrust and kick your limbs, and the walls began to close in. The umbilical cord still delivered all the food and oxygen you needed, but the bigger you got, the tighter the world became. Bliss turned into "no-exit terror." "I've got to get out of here," was probably one of your first conscious thoughts. (How many of us re-experience that same primal anxiety whenever a loving relationship seems constricting, claustrophobic or suffocating?) Thus you began the inevitable exit from Eden, the drama of separation, the panic of life and death!

The birth canal was a tight squeeze. You couldn't go back, and who knew what lay ahead? You twisted and turned, pressing with your head towards a distant freedom. Objectively, the distance you crossed was short, but the effort was enormous as each inch seemed like moving mountains. The pressure was unrelenting. The walls of your universe rumbled in tidal waves of upheaval. No wonder that, later in life, times of transition (changing jobs, moving or leaving a relationship) seem so traumatic. Sheer will power pushed you on. The will to live? The collective memory of ultimate deliverance? Who knows?

One thing seems certain. The pattern struggling to "make it" begins in the birth canal and continues through all our yearnings and longings in life, until released.

And then there was your mother's pain. Mother, your source of love and security for nine precious months, now contracting in fear and pain you never intended. "It's all going wrong. It wasn't supposed to be this way" (all-too-familiar thoughts in loving relationships). Your love was supposed to cause joy and celebration, not war and terror. Is love a mistake? Is life suffering? Is it better to hold love in, than cause the one we love such pain? In my opinion this *infant guilt syndrome* is responsible for many problems we create later in life. So long as you hold the idea that your life caused your mother pain, you will constantly engage your partners in primal warfare. Relationships become an emotional battle for survival. You think you need your partner to survive, resent him for it, and struggle to gain your independence. It seems that only one person can survive. It seems you have to leave relationships to continue your personal growth, just as you had to leave mother when it got too tight. The pain of separation seems the only alternative to the threat of suffocation. More on this later.

Birth, for most of us, was a rude awakening at best, and a terrible injustice at worst.

As rough as life was in the birth canal, deliverance was probably worse. If you were delivered in a hospital as I was, your birth was probably a function of your obstetrician's convenience as much as your mother's comfort. Nowadays there is great controversy over the proliferation of cesarian deliveries, the culmination of years and years of doctors making birth "easier."

In a sense, birth has become quite safe. The infant mortality rate has been greatly reduced, and premature babies who once could never be saved are being rescued with increasing regularity. We must acknowledge Western science for these significant developments.

But there is a great ignorance about birth; it is surrounded by a cloud of unconsciousness many doctors refuse to penetrate. Perhaps this cloud is a result of the anesthesia administered at birth; the collective unconsciousness around birth recapitulates the anesthesia of one's own birth. We now know that a chemical called *oxytocin* is released naturally at birth and that it produces a kind of forgetfulness about the experience.

As your first experience of this world, your entrance into life, and your initiation into reality, the significance of unravelling your birth trauma cannot be under-estimated!

The physical aspect of deliverance is a shock to consider, let alone experience. At birth you move from semi-darkness to brilliant lights, from quiet to noise, from womb warmth to relative coolness. Finally, as if this were not enough, the obstetrician probably handled you insensitively and cut your umbilical cord (your basis survival system) before you had a chance to cough up the amniotic fluid and teach yourself to breath. (No wonder you hold your breath whenever there's danger!)

If you weren't quick enough, the obstetrician probably flipped you upside down and gave you your first spanking, just to get you going. (Many of us develop a permanent tension pattern in our backs as a result.) The obstetrician! The first man who ever touched you, the first authority figure in your life, the first man in a uniform! No wonder you resist authorities so compulsively later on, yearning for someone to "save" you and, at the same time, resenting him for telling you what to do. "I can do it myself!" you cry.

The *obstetrician syndrome* is not the result of cruel and inhuman punishment; on the contrary, probably your obstetrician loved babies and was doing everything in his power to make sure you made it. The confusion of birth is a result of collective innocence and ignorance. Not content to leave well enough alone, your nurse probably took you from your mother and placed you in a nursery where you were just one of the crowd. Some birthday!

Birth is a time when the collective worldview of our culture is transmitted from generation to generation. The mother, the doctor, the nurse—all their birth traumas are activated as they wait, holding their breath, to see if you'll make it. And the moment you go into agreement with them, the collective worldview is assured further perpetuation. Many a doctor will justify the slapping of a newborn or its separation from its mother with the words "That's life!" As long as we think that life is cruel, the violence of traditional birth will be justified in our minds. As long as we believe that struggle is basic to human nature and that human nature is unalterable, the pleas for a more humane form of birth will go largely unnoticed.

Rebirthing

Before we can appreciate the insanity of conventional birth, we must heal ourselves of our fundamental paranoia and schizophrenia towards life. In other words, we must release the shock of our own births from our minds, bodies and spirits!

Primal therapy is an excellent tool for connecting you with primal rage and turning it into outrage. The challenge is that getting in touch with the rage is only the first step in releasing the hold of birth. Even at that, there is an ecstasy involved in the birth process that focusing on the pain can completely mask.

Rebirthing, a simple but subtly powerful breathing experience, puts you in touch with the pleasure of being alive and allows you to see your birth as an exciting, if confusing and frightening, interruption in the journey of your spirit into a wonderful world. Primal therapy puts you in outrage towards life. Rebirthing enables you to be outrageous—to get rage out and connect with the love that abounds in the universe.

In rebirthing all you actually do is lie down and breathe. You breathe and you breathe and you breathe and you breathe. For two hours or more you do "connected breathing." What happens is fairly astounding. On the most superficial levels, your body wakes up. That ancient numbness, the result of real and self-induced anesthesia, begins to melt away, and you begin to tingle, feel hot, cold, heavy, light, until the energy breaks through your resistance like a river breaking a dam and you feel enormous release and relaxation throughout your body.

Emotionally, rebirthing takes you through primal rage, the hurt and sadness beneath it, and that basic fear of surrender which creates the dilemma of love. Often you will see "pictures" of your birth or early childhood or remember prenatal sensations. The more you breathe, the more oxygen you carry through your bloodstream into the cells of your body. These cells function like the cells of a computer; once they are revived from their habitual numbness they contain a wealth of information that they are quite willing to transmit to your brain for remembering and release.

Rebirthing, of course, should be done in the presence of a professionally trained rebirther, the names of whom appear in the back of this book.

Sometimes people hear the word *rebirthing* and immediately think of being "reborn," an instantaneous spiritual transformation (usually through Christ) that some people report experiencing. Not so! Rebirthing is a cumulative process, not a one-time or one-month turnaround. To surrender in rebirthing is to surrender to the power of your breath as an ongoing transformational vehicle in your life.

Your breath is the bridge between the visible and invisible worlds; it is the point of exchange between what you take in and what you let out, the point at which thought gives form to spirit. In your breathing you reveal your basic attitudes towards life itself, and, in the course of rebirthing, your breath naturally restores itself to the balance and harmony it would have known all along, had it not been for the trauma of the first breath. In rebirthing you release the panic of the first breath. The result is that you experience breathing as a spontaneous, cleansing rhythm rather than as a fearful, controlled machine. Normally stressful situations, produce an intuitive sigh of release instead of breath-taking panic. Relationships, so often controlled by the subconscious fear of separation (the memory of leaving the womb) become easier, safer, more pleasurable and committed.

The pulse of the universe becomes the pulse of your breath as well as of your heart. As your breath opens, your heart opens. Rebirthing is a peak experience of life and love available with a minimum of effort and relatively little cost. Moreover, its results are lasting. Rebirthing is the invisible key to your heart.

Write out a birth report, including the following information: name, date of birth, parents' ages at birth, siblings' ages, and whether you were cesarian, premature, breach, induced, incubator, late, cord around neck, or any other unusual circumstances. If you cannot remember or find out this information, do not worry. Often the memories come up during rebirthing, and sometimes they are released from the body without the mind's seeing the pictures. It doesn't matter—you feel the difference nonetheless. Call a rebirther to discuss your birth and see if rebirthing is for you.

Of course, every birth is an individual event, unique and incomparable. You may have been premature, breach, cesarian, induced or late. You may have been born with the cord around your neck or been put in an incubator. The particular physical and emotional conditions at the time of your birth caused you to form conclusions which comprise your Primal Law and your basic attitudes toward life. You survived your birth and you've survived your life thus far, so you know what you're using works for you. But it may be time for things to work more easily, to shed a layer of toughness and surrender into a more gentle and loving way of being. Rebirthing can certainly help you to do this.

Chapter VII

Guilt,
the mafia
of the mind

Since most people think there is something wrong with them, or they've done something wrong, they don't believe they deserve love. Often they will subconsciously sabotage the love they do receive!

Guilt, like the serpent in Eden, is the sneakiest and most subtle of all negative patterns. Often you don't feel guilty when you act it. The reason for this is that guilt is not a feeling so much as a condition. Guilt, in fact, is an avoidance of feeling.

Guilt is the condition of separation. It is the opposite of grace. Guilt is the moat protecting the ego's castle!

Psychologically, guilt is the great saboteur of life. It is why we don't let ourselves experience "having it all." When you're guilty, you're messing up your life in some area because you subconsciously feel unworthy of complete success. You finally get that perfect job and your car breaks down; you repair your car and your house burns down; you buy your perfect house and your relationship falls apart. Your life is a sinking ship, and every time you plug a hole a new leak springs. A guilty person always finds a way to make something go wrong in his life to reflect his Primal Law ("There's something wrong with me" or "I'm unworthy") and thereby confirm his worst fear about himself.

Guilt causes people who become successful overnight to destroy their success, if not themselves. Their consciousness cannot reconcile their sudden fame and fortune with their past low self-esteem. They either make a leap in consciousness or fall off the deep end.

Guilt is the mafia of the mind! It is a protection plan we sell ourselves in order to avoid anticipated punishment. The only problem is that this particular form of protection involves self-punishment. All guilt is masochistic. The thought is "If only I suffer enough, I'll be forgiven!" "If only I punish myself enough, maybe people will take pity on me and not hurt me!" Guilt is based on the illusion that pain is redemption, rather than innocence. Guilt makes martyrs think they are saints. Guilt is the godfather masquerading as God!

In New Mexico I came across a religious sect called *Penitentes*. They practice self- flagellation, and even crucifixion, as a way to God. The truth is, no matter how well you punish yourself, guilt is never really satisfied until you receive "a good licking." Then it causes you to gloat in your suffering, self-righteously defending your addiction to pain.

Finally, guilt is not content until you make the supreme sacrifice of your life. In your death your ego laughs and dances on your grave. It has proven you unworthy of life. You were, after all, a sinner!

The causes of guilt are multiple and mutually re-enforcing. The infant guilt syndrome, referred to earlier, is based on the erroneous conclusion that you hurt your mother at birth. Out of your love for her, you "take on" her pain, making a silent pact with yourself to suffer for those you love as a way of protecting them from the pain you expect to cause them and, at the same time, safeguarding yourself from any possible retaliation. You suppress your aliveness whenever you feel intimacy approaching. You close your heart and hold yourself in, becoming increasingly uncomfortable, claustrophobic and suffocated, and then either exploding in primal rage or leaving in primal terror—in both cases re-enacting the drama of infant guilt and abandonment.

Guilt is separation insurance!

The popular "outgrowth" myth springs from pre- and perinatal guilt. This is the absurd idea that one partner can outgrow a relationship, as though a relationship were a pot you plant yourself in. It was in the womb you decided that you have to leave in order to continue your personal growth, and that the journey meant pain, panic, fear and loss. No wonder transitions tend to be such stressful times for us.

In the womb you gradually grew until your mother's space could no longer contain and nourish you. Paradise suddenly became hell. You were boxed in and had to leave to survive. So you chose to get out. Then the obstetrician cut your umbilical cord before you learned how to use your lungs, and your first breath was full of pain and panic. In relationships you often relive this same emotional sequence. You move from the bliss of new love to a gradual feeling of constriction and claustrophobia. It often seems like paradise has become living hell and that leaving the relationship is your only salvation. The only alternative is to play your mother's role and push your partner out. Often it becomes increasingly difficult to breathe around your lover and you will find yourself opening the window on cold winter nights so you can get enough air. (Probably your partner will want the window shut.)

The result of all this is The Great Double Bind of most relationships: the feeling that you can't live with your partner and can't survive without him. So the fear of love and the fear of loss are joined in holy matrimony with Father Guilt performing the ceremony, smiling as still another unsuspecting couple bites the dust.

You forget that your heart is out of the womb, that the cord has been cut, and that you are only limited by your own mind and your unwillingness to use a little imagination in living.

You also forget that you never really hurt your mother at birth; her pain was the result of her own birth trauma—her fear of reliving the intensity of her birth caused her to hold on and hurt.

Under the anesthesia is pain; under the pain is fear; under the fear is hurt. But under that hurt is joy. The only way to heal this basic hurt and get to the joy is to surrender to love and to see that you create your own pain and pleasure, as others do theirs. The tragic guilt at birth is a loving infant absorbing its loving mother's suffering.

Guilt is hereditary. At every birth the terrible torch is passed on. Born guilty, you tend to gravitate towards punishment. As a child you experience disapproval—your parents' criticizing, judging and evaluating you—as their parents did them. This *parental disapproval syndrome,* commonly called "family tradition," cements your infant guilt, causing you to retreat into your mind and wonder what people will think of you before you act. You learn to deny your intuition in favor of pleasing the minds of people you think you need to survive. Of course, you secretly resent these people and tend to blame them for your own pattern of selling out.

Make a list of ten things you think you've done to hurt others, e.g. hitting someone, withholding your love or lying. Then make a second list of ten things you think others have done to hurt you. Now breathe, and take a long look at your two lists. Release your primal guilt by forgiving yourself for acting out the subconscious desire of other guilty minds for punishment. And forgive yourself for attracting punishment to alleviate the pain of your own guilt. See that no one is ever at fault, that guilt and punishment are always seeking each other out, pattern attracting pattern, victim and victimizer in unspoken agreement.

You forget that your guilt is in search of a villain who will make you feel like a helpless victim. Your guilt thinks that helplessness is innocence.

Innocence can neither be created nor destroyed. It either is or is not. I prefer to see innocence to guilt. It's more pleasing to the eye and soothing to the heart. I prefer to see the God in children and the child in each of us. If we act like little devils once in a while, it is only a case of sheep in wolf's clothing.

☆ *You can begin to forgive yourself for pretending to be guilty.*

You can begin to acknowledge that the innocence you see in a child's eyes is your own. How can you see what you're not?

Every journey through the birth canal recapitulates the expulsion of Adam and Eve from Eden. Religious guilt and religious "education" substantiates the suppression of aliveness from birth as well as living with disapproving parents.

Most religions teach us that we are sinners, that we are bad, corrupt, fallen angels. Although you may have resented hearing this and rebelled from it, the thought that God has condemned you might be lurking in the cavern of your subconscious mind. And probably the more you were told you were bad as a child, the more you chose to act bad to get even. Or else, you chose the long and winding path back to God, which your initial thought of separation prevents you from ever completing in your heart.

You become a professional seeker, longing to attain a union that can only come from surrendering to your innocence. You attach your basic struggle pattern to a spiritual quest, searching for the right teacher, therapist, guru to save you. Only the more you seek, the more you face yourself. The basic dilemma of love follows you like a shadow every step of your quest.

There is no escape from yourself. There is no escape from freedom. The prison is just your own mind.

Social guilt is the most popular form of self-denial. You could even call it a fad or a trend. Social guilt is very "in" and, like rock and roll, it claims to be here to stay. Acting on social guilt, you must think of all the starving children in the world before feasting on luscious steak, or consider all the homeless refugees before purchasing your dream house.

This line of reasoning causes you to think it's a sin to win at life as long as others are losing, as though your success somehow magically takes away from others. Following this logic we'd be left with a world of losers, each of whom had to wait for everyone else to win before making a move himself. We'd be stuck in a state of planetary paralysis.

The causative beliefs behind social guilt are (1) "expressing myself hurts others; therefore I must hold myself back," (clearly, a spinoff from birth), and (2) "there is real scarcity on the planet, so the more I have, the less others have, and that's not fair." The latter belief leads to a Robin Hood or Marxist view of life, both of which make for interesting reading but are basically grounded in fantasy.

There is no scarcity.

There is more than enough for everyone to have more than enough.

The fact is, there is no lack except in our minds. Buckminster Fuller, for one, has scientifically demonstrated the natural abundance of wealth on the planet. There is clearly more than enough for everyone to live very well indeed. The real problems are attitudinal, which causes a worldwide withholding pattern. Planetary relationships reflect family patterns.

Social guilt proclaims the rich to be bad guys and the poor, the victims. You begin to think that money corrupts and subconsciously limit your success, or hide it, in order to protect your innocence.

There are at least as many corrupt poor people as wealthy ones. Money isn't evil; money is just currency—a medium of exchange. In exchanging money for goods or services, you can communicate love or resentment, depending on your thoughts.

☆ *To succeed is not to deprive others but to inspire them.* Moreover, the more you succeed, the more you are able to contribute to the well-being of others. The only way you can succeed is to share your talents and make a useful contribution to people's lives. And the only thing you can do with the money you receive from your contribution is to contribute more—by spending it, saving it or investing it. Money has no value except in circulation. Even in a bank it gets "used," invested to support individuals or businesses that, in turn, support individuals.

Wealthy people deserve love too!

You can have compassion without taking on people's pain.

Imagine a world free of social guilt. Close your eyes and take a breath and imagine a world of people free of fear and able to express themselves fully, using all their God-given talents to make affirmative contributions to the well-being of others. Close your eyes and embrace this vision in your heart.

A world without guilt is a planet of self-reliant individualists cooperating rather than competing to make the most of both internal and external resources.

Make *a list of ten ways you experience your innocence, whether it's eating ice cream, bathing or going to amusement parks. Schedule these activities into your calendar. Now.*

If this sounds like a pipe dream, it is only because you are so addicted to your mind's illusion of guilt and separation. How can you ever recapture your innocence when, in your mind, it is a paradise permanently lost, an irretrievable womb, a home you can never go home to?

Your innocence is never more than one thought away! In forgiving yourself completely, you come to see your inherent goodness. Your heart opens and you realize you can trust your intuition, that even your guilt and suffering were based on love, however misapplied.

★ *Often we confuse guilt and conscience, thinking we should listen to the voice of guilt in order to live a life of integrity. Guilt is your mind disapproving of your heart. Conscience is your heart reminding your mind of what you really value. They are quite opposite states, though your ego can confuse you into thinking you have a "guilty conscience."*

Your conscience is never guilty. It is the voice of wisdom that drives your guilt up and out, restoring your innocence to its natural throne.

Since guilt is a function of self-disapproval, the antidote is a heavy dose of self-love and forgiveness. You're usually guilty about failing, succeeding, judging, feeling; the remedy is to accept all these aspects of yourself and stop using them to demonstrate your Primal Law.

However, if your conscience is bothering you, no amount of forgiveness or acceptance will, in itself, make you feel better. For example, if you are a compulsive liar and your conscience reminds you to tell the truth, forgiving yourself for lying is not enough. You must then choose to break the habit by telling the truth. You must be willing to change your behavior.

If you feel guilty for succeeding, forgiveness is sufficient. On the other hand, if your conscience tells you to pay your taxes and you forgive yourself for failing to do so, that's only half the process. You then must pay your taxes. (Maybe you're trying to avoid paying because taxes and death seem married in your mind.)

Integrity is that which produces wholeness in your life; integrity is the result of integrating your spiritual self into your everyday behavior.

Lack of integrity is that which disintegrates wholeness—it causes a falling apart of your life. It is therefore practical to obey the suggestions of your conscience. It is only God telling you what is good for you, what will make you happier.

Conscience is your perfect personal consultant. It is your guardian angel.

If conscience is the voice of goodness in your heart, what is good? According to the dictionary, *good* means: "suitable, beneficial, real, healthy, happy, sufficient, worthy." *Bad* is: "not good, not as it should be, unfavorable, spoiled, faulty, unhealthy."

Good is that which leads us to the highest good, call it love, God, the greatest good for the greatest number. Good is also that which furthers our mental, physical and spiritual well-being. Evil is that which takes us off the path. Goodness is the route to our innermost perfect spirit, and evil is the direction away from spirit, love and creative energy. You might think of good as the creative power in the universe and evil as the perversion of that power for destructive purposes.

Good is what opens the heart; bad is what shuts it down!

Make an integrity check list! List the major areas of your life: relationships (are you telling the truth, loving yourself and respecting others?), work (are you making a contribution to the best of your ability; are you receiving the money you deserve; are you at the right job?), home (are you keeping your living space in order?), health (are you taking care of your body?), and so on. Check this list daily and make it your intention to score 100 percent. When you neglect an area, forgive yourself, figure out why, and re-commit to doing what makes you feel good.

The Garden of Eden story is about the origin of good and evil. As long as Adam and Eve ate from the Tree of Life, they were fine. They were in integrity because they were being nourished by Life itself, which is good, whole, complete and perfect. When they chose to eat of the Tree of the Knowledge of Good and Evil, they made a fundamental mistake in their thinking. They assumed (1) they were separate from God and that knowledge was the way to overcome separation; (2) evil was a subject worth studying and that life was not good, sufficient and complete, which it is. Therefore, since thought is creative, they created more evil to study. *That's what temptation is: drawing more evil to you, pretending it's a worthwhile pursuit.* Being expelled from the Garden was simply the logical result of choosing to study evil, which does not exist in paradise. The ingredients of evil are sorrow, misery, pain, disease and death, none of which existed in Eden. Sin entails punishment because *sin is separating ourselves, or missing the mark (as in archery) of our essential goodness.* Sin is wrong-thinking resulting in wrong direction!

The ways back to good are, first of all, to recognize the errors in your thoughts and deeds. Life is essentially a series of love lessons. If you are not happy, interrogate your mind until you discover and reverse your "bad" thinking. Realize that all apparent obstacles are only opportunities to grow in disguise. Recognize evil for what it is: rebellion from the good life. Satan was the first rebel.

This is a call for all prodigal sons and daughters to come home again. You can. Until you come home to your heart, the door to the world is closed to you.

Choose the path of good deeds: kindness, generosity, forgiveness, love. The purpose of good deeds is not to get approval or earn love. *The real purpose of good deeds is to express, expand, and evolve your essentially good spirit.* Evolution, in its highest sense, is the result of good deeds, and the reason for this is that good deeds create integrity, while bad deeds create disintegration, destruction and death. Good thoughts, words and deeds support the increasing alignment and integration of your mind, body and spirit.

Acknowledge that Good is what is real, that Evil is an illusion not worth pursuing and very dangerous.

★ Think of it this way: there is Divine Law, Spiritual Law and Physical Law. Evolution moves from the Divine to the Spiritual to the Physical, then back to the Divine.

According to Divine Law, you are always good and perfect, and it is inevitable that all spirits attain this realization.

According to Spiritual Law, thought is creative, you have a free choice and you can create or destroy as you so choose.

According to Physical Law, every action has a reaction, every cause an effect.

Physical Law governs the realm of behavior, and the more you choose to bring your everyday behavior into alignment with Divine Law, the more you experience integrity in your life.

Goodness is the essence of love, and an open heart is a good heart, healthy, happy and wise.

Make a list of all the good deeds you are willing to do in the next month, and commit yourself to doing them by scheduling them into your calendar.

Implants on Guilt

I am innocent!

I forgive myself for thinking I was separate.

I forgive myself for pretending to be guilty.

I forgive myself for my addiction to my Primal Law.

I forgive myself for thinking I caused pain at my birth.

I forgive myself completely.

I am the source of pleasure and pain in my life, and everyone else is in theirs.

My intention is loving.

My love is good enough for me and everyone else.

My aliveness is a healing force on the planet.

My pleasure pleasures others, and if it doesn't, so what.

I love myself, and other people are not my problem.

I can have compassion for others without taking on their pain.

The more I win, the more others win. The more others win, the more I win. Therefore, I am winning more and more all the time.

I don't have to sin to win.

The more I win, the more I feel my innocence.

I don't have to lose to win.

I am completely lovable, whether I win or lose.

People are safe in my presence.

Since people are safe in my presence, they don't need my protection.

Since I am safe in the presence of others, I am free to express myself fully.

I deserve to be wealthy and prosperous.

My wealth contributes to everyone's well-being, and everyone's wealth contributes to my well-being.

I am good natured.

My love always hits its target.

I deserve to have it all.

Chapter VIII

Conflicted
Hearts

Most of us are blessed with strong hearts, resilient to the changes of fortune that are, after all, a part of everyone's life. When your heart is open, you move through these changes, experiencing your feelings, learning more about who you are and how to get what you want in life. Your heart grows stronger in the process.

When you integrate the lessons of these changes, you become a healthy adult, as opposed to a functioning grown-up. Unfortunately, as you go through the normal stages of growth, you usually run into some changes that seem too much to handle—overwhelming changes that may resemble the unrelenting intensity of birth, changes you shrink from experiencing, let alone integrating. The result is your heart becomes fragmented, and pain prevents you from feeling the wholeness you desire. Often we'd rather hold onto this old pain because it is familiar and seems to protect us from the threat of the unknown.

A heart attack is an attack of heart!

In our relationships, the more love we receive, the more the old pain is activated for the purpose of release. If you're too afraid to let your old wounds show, the pain and the love clash and the result is conflict.

☆ *A conflicted heart is one in which the desire to surrender and the fear of loss are deadlocked.*

Most of these conflicts are lodged in old patterns—bad habits rooted in negative programs from our childhood. Anyone committed to an open heart has chosen to uproot these programs and replace them with new outlooks. You will therefore tend to remember and relive the stages of your growth that are least resolved and integrated. Growth is a progression through regression. Sometimes it feels like you are backsliding into experiences and feelings you've devoted a lot of energy to putting behind you. Not so. You can recover your past without being overwhelmed by it. In fact, the thought of overwhelm was what caused you to shut down in the first place. Life never gives you more than you can handle.

Life never gives you more than you can handle.

As infants, children and adolescents we learn by imitating. We are born actors and have an instinctive know-how for copying the ways of the people we love in order to please them. We play house, we play doctor, we play Cowboys and Indians. And more profoundly, if subconsciously, we play the soap operas and situation comedies of our parents' relationships.

In matters of the heart, our parents are obviously our first role models. We tend to copy in our adult relationships the ways they related to each other and the ways they related to us. Or else we rebel compulsively from their ways. Since what we resist hangs on the longest, we end up with our parents anyway. (I know I swore I'd never be with anyone like mother. So when I grew up, I attracted women who didn't seem anything like her. Then I'd struggle to change my partner into my mother so I could take out my resentment on her. Not until I forgave my mother completely and became friends with her did this pattern dissolve entirely.)

In other words, the problems we perceived in our parents' relationship with each other and with us become our problems. We take on these problems because (1) we love our parents, (2) we want to save our parents, (3) we want to please our parents, and (4) our parents' way is the only way we know as children.

You cannot bond with a mate until you set your parents free.

You can, if you are a man, attract a woman who resembles your mother or father, depending with which you are most unresolved. Similarly, if you are a woman, your chosen man could express the qualities of your mother or father. Or perhaps your mate is a mixture of what is unresolved with each parent. You can also find yourself alternating from mother to father in successive relationships—in an effort to balance your own female and male qualities.

The point at which we shut down our hearts to our parents, or they to us or each other, becomes the point at which our hearts close to those we love.

☆ *What you don't like about your partner is frequently what you haven't forgiven your parents for.*

Make *four separate lists: (1) five problems in your parents' relationship, (2) five problems in your mother's relationship with you as a child, (3) five problems in your father's relationship with you as a child, and (4) five problems in your most recent relationship. Notice the patterns.*

Case I

You are a woman whose father worked late, came home exhausted, and buried himself in the newspaper or TV, where he fell asleep every night. Your perception of the situation was that your father neglected you, never giving you the attention you wanted. You grow up and attract a series of men all of whom are workaholics who (you feel) neglect you. In your mind you can never get the attention you need from a man because you never got it in the first place. You are stuck in *past neglect.* In fact, your love and loyalty for your father makes you addicted to neglect. If a man begins to give to you the attention you consciously seek, you will reject him, avoid him or just plain not be interested in him. You will play the neglecting parent. Subconsciously you prefer neglect because, much as it hurt you, it reminds you of father. There's no place like home. Also, the neglect enables you to feel the pain you want to release.

Case II

You are a man whose mother was an alcoholic. Your pattern as an adult is to attract women who (1) are alcoholics, (2) enjoy drinking occasionally but, in your mind, have a serious drinking problem. You attract what you are accustomed to, and if the behavior doesn't fit your picture you project the picture on the behavior. You see women in terms of alcohol; you are constantly focusing on anything in their behavior that might be construed to be addictive. Secretly, you want to save your mother, but it is hopeless. The less your partner drinks, the less she reminds you of your mother and the more your disappointment emerges. Maybe you start drinking then. Or perhaps you finally find a woman who has never touched alcohol in her life, but before long she is devouring huge amounts of alcohol and doesn't even know why. It happens that her father disapproved of her and she has subconscious need to draw disapproval out of you. She loves you so much she'll do anything to get you to disapprove of her. Even drink.

Case III

You are a woman who was abused as a child. Your father was conflicted and angry, and your innocence reminded him of everything he thought he had lost. It drove him wild, and he beat you, usually when you were most alive and happy. Your perception at the time was that love equals abuse. Also, your primal guilt was re-enforced. If your father, the man you most loved, beat you, surely there must be something wrong with you. You develop a subconscious addiction to pain and punishment.

You grow up and, consciously, the last thing in the world you want is a hostile man. You look for a caring, gentle man. Unfortunately, your secret desire for punishment causes you to attract men with tremendous suppressed hostility. The more you love these "gentle" men, the more you trigger what is unresolved within them. Your love is so powerful and your drive to heal your father so strong that you are never satisfied until your man "gets in touch" with his feelings, which, in your mind, translates into violent explosions, his rage strangely vindicating both your guilt and resentment. You get to be right in your perception "Men hurt me!"

Obviously, you tend to attract men who have a fair amount of unexpressed hostility, probably towards their mother. Your love reminds them of their smothering mother and their primal rage causes them to fight you rather than surrender.

Case IV

You are a woman whose parents were divorced when you were three. Your father fell in love with another woman and you never saw him again. You grew up with your mother, thinking it was you who caused the separation. In your perception, your presence causes separation and the man you love always leaves.

You grow up and find you are able to have wonderful, loving relationships with men that tend to last two to three years. But the closer you approach the three-year limit, the more active is your subconscious need to create separation. Consciously, you want a long-lasting relationship, but your secret addiction to guilt and separation sabotages you. As the three-year limit closes in, your partner becomes attracted to other women. Eventually, he falls in love and leaves, just like good old dad.

The point at which your parents seemed to withdraw their physical affection from you is the point at which you tend to cause separation in your adult relationships. The gravitational pull of family tradition should not be underestimated. Your perception that your love divides people, that you always come between people to get love and that men leave you forms the foundation of a typical incest pattern. You will always find yourself entangled in triangle relationships, either attracted to married men or drawing in another woman to compete for your man.

The major patterns that seem to cause conflicted hearts are: struggle, guilt, disapproval, helplessness, revenge and incest.

Sometimes these patterns seem hopelessly embedded in our personalities and we think we'll never be free of them. It is important to remember that patterns are not cosmic webs in which you are trapped; patterns are just old choices in your subconscious mind, bad habits of the heart, nostalgia for the past. Since a pattern is unconscious, becoming aware of it is the first step in transformation.

Saying no to what you don't want opens the door to what you do want.

The second step is to notice the power of the addiction to the past. Recognize the safety in what is familiar. Even if you think it's not what you want, you know you can survive men leaving you; furthermore, the familiar feelings of self-pity and loneliness are home base to you. Your Primal Law feels very real at this level of addiction and sometimes surrendering to, rather than resisting, the experience of it can do more for releasing it, especially if your are then willing to breathe and change your mind.

Third, you must let go of the past. Often it feels as if the past is holding onto you, but this is never the case. You are not a victim! You know you are the one holding and that you can use that same energy to let go and let new love in.

☆ *Holding on to what you don't want is a sure way to keep out what you do want!*

Frequently, we were so hurt as children that our choice was to get even forever. And to strike first! The revenge pattern, as with other patterns, can and usually does become covert. If your perception as a child was that life is a series of attacks, you might easily have grown into a vindictive person. Your pattern is to seduce others into loving you, then launch major offenses at those people. Your thoughts are that you can't trust anyone, that you'll never forgive your parents, and that sadism is more satisfying than masochism. You see life as a rat race, and you'll be the first one across the finish line, no matter what. You'd rather be a victimizer than a victim, as if there were any fundamental difference.

If you're stuck in revenge and attract someone who is determined to love you, you'll really have your hands full. You will do anything to destroy the love before the love destroys the pattern. You will disapprove, avoid, neglect or even strike a partner if the love feels threatening enough. The irony is that the only thing love ever threatens is pain—it wants to flush out old pain. But in your mind to feel the pain is to be vulnerable to attack again, and you've already chosen your system of defense.

The choice to forgive and not to retaliate is the pivotal point in transformation. The choice to share your hurt, not your anger, is the choice to love again. And the more you focus on the reality of your heart connection with your partner, the more the illusion of separation disappears. And when the separation dissolves, so do the separating patterns.

People resist what they most desire.

The fourth step in releasing negative programs is to notice and be honest about your fear of change. If you are accustomed to abandonment, having a partner who refuses to leave is a major "confront." It doesn't compute in your mind or heart. If you are attracted to men with no money because your father was poor, having a prosperous man love you will definitely shake you up, making you extremely uncomfortable, sad and even angry. You will feel as if you are betraying family tradition.

This is why we resist what we most desire: To let it in feels like cutting the cord to your own personal history, which, however warped, is still known. At this point it can feel as if you might actually disappear if you let go. The fear of the unknown often plunges us back into the darkness of the birth canal and our deep mistrust of any form of deliverance.

The fifth step in transformation is really going for what you want, not waiting until you complete the past. Go for it even when your mind is saying no, no, no. Going for success in life is the quickest route to completing the past. The more you put your heart's energy behind your spirit's real desires, the more you break through the prison of your past.

The Heart Connection

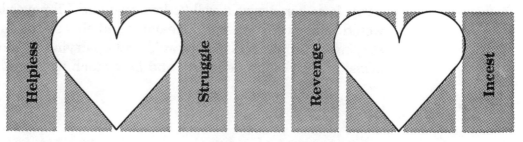

Focusing on the love dissolves the patterns!

Get clear on what you really want. Don't be vague. And set yourself on a path in the right direction. If you're not clear on what you want, you won't recognize it when it comes along. You'll be too busy looking for the old familiar attractions of your mind.

Surround yourself with a family of loving people who support your growth, not your addiction to misery. Be willing to be accountable to these people, especially when they don't fit your pictures of friends because they don't support your lies about yourself. Group support is essential in transforming your experience of yourself in family, and since family is the origin of all your relationships, true healing starts there.

Relationships tend to go through the birth/death cycle the same way people do. If you're stuck in the fear of loss, you will subconsciously withdraw your heart from available love, carefully observing all signs of decay and secretly waiting for the worst to happen. It is often those who most fear loss who leave first, either emotionally or physically. People who can't stay in a relationship are usually the ones who most fear abandonment. They don't want to experience intimacy because when they are left they have to feel the old pain they're still angry about. So they both get even and avoid feeling by leaving first. *The leaving pattern is the one that causes relationships to end.*

I remember, in my relationship with my wife Mallie, when the death urge came up, it was a powerful and brutal force that almost consumed us. It was the point at which all my previous relationships had broken down, the point at which leaving seemed inevitable. There were two major things I did to overcome this pattern that might be of value to you. First, whenever the "leaving" energy came up in my body, no matter how strongly I felt Mallie pushing me away from her, I would yell "I love you and I'll never leave you!" I would take all that energy of leaving and choose the thought of staying to project it. Usually we'd end up crying in each other's arms, acknowledging our love and how much we feared losing it.

Second, we played a game that consisted of spending twenty-four hours in physical contact. It was a wild, funny, difficult game to play, but we sensed that to win the game all we had to do was play it. We went to a party. Arm in arm, the force of separation tugged at us from all directions. We drew in other women, other men, distractions from all over, acting out our thought of separation. It was a crazy dance we did that night, but we held on, asserting our will to surrender until it drove out the demon of loss. Then, suddenly, the divisive energy ebbed. It disappeared as mysteriously as it had first appeared. We were one again. A heart connection between two conscious people can overcome any negative thought!

Different people tend to get stuck at different stages of growth. One person is angry from a prenatal experience of attempted abortion; another is deeply depressed because his mother died giving birth to him; a third is suffering from her parents' divorce when she was six. Learning how to communicate your love to people often depends on where they are, psychologically and emotionally, as well as on you.

It is not always appropriate or even possible to find out what events shaped a particular personality, but your intuition can provide you with all the information you need. Having your heart open enables you to "read" a person emotionally. The stages of growth can be generally characterized, but each person is a unique individual traveling his own journey in life. In opening yourself to yourself, you receive the knowledge of others. And the more you recognize where others are in their own minds, the more you can keep your heart open and realize their behavior has little to do with you.

When we stop taking others so personally, we feel free to be ourselves and share love, letting the seeds land where they will. The clearer you get, the more you provide a natural clearing space for others. You begin to love people and watch them let go with you. You become an open heart therapist when you experience the healing power of love and choose to love others unconditionally. When your heart stays open no matter what your mind is doing, you experience major miracles every day of your life. Indeed, miracles become commonplace.

The Stages of Release

I

Notice what's happening.

The men I love leave me.

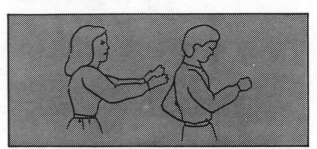

II

Notice your addiction.

Poor me! I'll never keep a man.

III

Forgive the past

1. Forgive yourself for creating it.

2. Forgive your mother completely.

3. Forgive your father completely.

IV

Notice your fear of change.

A man who wants to stay terrifies me.

V

Go for it!

I'll choose who I want and go through the fear.

Chapter IX

Love
Yourself
no matter
what

You've seen him walking down the street—strong, safe and self-reliant. He emanates a confidence and certainty you've always admired, perhaps even envied. Yet he is not cocky. He is poised, open and ready for the moment. His trust in life makes worry and anxiety unnecessary. He is calm, yet brimming with aliveness. His body is relaxed, but not at all sluggish. His eyes are clear and his smile is genuine. Here is a man who is comfortable with his past, knows where he's going and enjoys where he's at. Who is this person? Could he be you?

The key to unlocking your unlimited potential is love. Love alone sets you free; love alone heals you; and love begins with you alone. There is no point in looking outside yourself for what you haven't given yourself in the first place. Love begins at home! You will never find your perfect date, let alone mate, if you haven't become your own perfect partner.

So often I hear people say "I hate myself for being like that," "I hate myself for doing that," "I hate myself for saying that." Hating yourself for what you wish were otherwise inhibits the growth process. Hate is counter-productive. No matter what you think, say or do, you always deserve your own love and respect. You can learn your lessons in life without hating yourself for your "problems."

As you overcome your guilt, you begin to feel you deserve a whole lot more.

As you begin to see this world as a reward instead of a punishment, you realize there must be something very wonderful about you that you find yourself in such an incredible amusement park, namely life.

As your heart opens, you begin to experience the infinite reservoir of love at your disposal, and suddenly you can appreciate how extraordinary it is to be alive. Many of us take life for granted, rarely stopping to note that as long as we are alive we are in possession of the most precious gift in the universe, life itself. It is the gift from which all other gifts come, the gift we wouldn't trade for all the money in the world.

Just think about that for a minute: You already own something more valuable to you than all the riches in the world!

An attitude of gratitude for being alive is the first ingredient in the recipe for self-esteem. The more connected you feel to your choice to be alive, the more correct you feel in your choice. What good taste you have! Life, what an excellent choice! Clearly you are *choosing* life as long as you do not choose death. Your life urge is stronger than your death urge. How wonderful!

As you think of yourself, so you are thought of by others.

You really cannot give more love to others than you give yourself, nor can you receive more love than you receive from yourself. You alone are the source of love in your life. The people you meet are always a perfect reflection of what you think and how you feel about yourself.

If you are still clinging to the thought that there is someone out there, some knight in shining armor or fair damsel who will swoop you off your feet, sending you head over heels and solving all your problems, forget it! This romantic quest is a fiction—a hopeless search for fantasy fulfillment, a longing to recreate the umbilical cord, to find the perfect parental substitute. There is no Mr. or Ms. Right out there! Only you!

Become your own perfect partner. You are Mr. Right!

No one can fill the void in you but you!

Besides, if someone loves you more than you love yourself, you will only push him away, avoid him or think he is lying. Or else you will struggle to earn the love you think you don't deserve.

And if you love someone beyond his love for himself, he will reject you or struggle to get you to reject him. Or you will try to change him and he will resent you. Or he will change to please you, then leave you.

Unconditional love, like charity, begins at home. You cannot bring the love to others that you've neglected to bring yourself. Begin by being kind to yourself. Begin by acknowledging yourself.

*S*elf-esteem profile! At the top of a piece of paper write the following statement: "What I am is . . ." and list all the qualities, positive and negative, you associate with yourself. Fill up the entire page, free-associating, not worrying about whether they are true or not. When you are done, underline all those characteristics you consider positive. You are looking at a profile of the current state of your self-esteem. The "negative" qualities are those things you want to forgive yourself for, or reverse through implanting new thoughts.

Take a plunge into your own perfection!

In a sense your identity is a function of two ships passing in the night. Only one of the ships isn't going anywhere. It's already there—the constant, never-changing perfect you! This is the part of you that knows you already know, the impartial observer, the key witness, the part that notices "Oh, you're doing that again," but does not judge. The other ship is on the move, enduring storms, avoiding icebergs, correcting its course, seeking a destination.

You are both of these ships—one constant and perfect, the other changing and imperfect. One part is as solid as a rock, the other is water continually flowing over the rock. Keys to life are remembering your perfect loving core, accepting your changing, imperfect shell, and learning how to change course in midstream when you discover you're moving against the current.

Self-acceptance is the first step to self-esteem: To accept yourself in all your apparent ambiguity and contradiction, to allow yourself to be who you are without judgment, creates a context for loving others unconditionally.

Self-respect is the second step: To respect yourself wherever you are in your life, whatever your apparent limitations seem to be, can be a springboard for quantum leaps.

Self-respect can open the door to divine intuition. Perhaps you don't trust yourself enough. Perhaps you look for other people to give you instructions in life, but because you don't trust yourself you have no real trust to extend to others. You are stuck between your helplessness and your mistrust, knowing that until you can rely on your own intuition you will always be suspicious of others, much as you seek out their advice!

Do not blame yourself for doubting others. Not everyone is completely trustworthy, and you are probably just reflecting other people's doubts about themselves. *Different people are dependable for different things. One of the keys to successful relationships is knowing whom to trust for what, when.* Most successful business people know this.

Maybe you think you should trust everyone all the time. Nonsense! It is safe and appropriate to trust your own mistrust. Paranoia can be healthy in realistic doses.

You don't have to be naive to be loving. True love is never blind. True love sees the truth and speaks it, knowing that the truth is always liberating, even when it sounds like "I just don't trust you." Whenever you speak the truth, your self-esteem is served and so is the well-being of others, no matter how it looks. Trust the truth of each moment!

"No, thank you" is a loving response.

Giving and taking no for an answer can often be a conflict for the heart. It need not be. A good friend can always accept a no.

Saying yes when you mean no is betraying yourself and will cause your self-esteem to plummet. Often the fear of saying no is the fear of hurting someone. You want to protect this person from the pain. This guilt causes you either to shut down your heart and sound angry when saying no, or else to say yes out of obligation, only to resent it later.

Take out a clean sheet of paper. Write at the top: "The things I want to acknowledge myself for are..." and make a list of at least 25 things for which you are willing to approve of yourself. Don't be meek; don't be self-effacing. Give yourself permission to sing your own praises for awhile. Remember, whatever you've created in the past, you *were* the creator, and you deserve to acknowledge your own creativity no matter what.

You can say no with loving energy behind it. People don't really want you to say yes when you mean no. It is disrespectful of them. When you do it, they get a double message which makes them feel confused and uncomfortable about receiving.

Of course, you too have to learn to take no for an answer. Perhaps one of your motives in saying yes too much to others is that you want to protect yourself from all the no's you fear hearing. It seems as though we all have a rejection quota, and when we get rejected enough we stop rejecting ourselves, and then others begin accepting us more fully.

All rejection is acceptance in disguise!

Most people never get through their rejection quota because they live in such fear and hopelessness that they rarely even risk asking for what they want. They hold themselves back with the thought that they're protecting themselves, but all they're really protecting is their fear. To get through the fear of rejection it is necessary to make a habit of asking for what you want. If you get no for an answer, locate and release the negative thought someone is agreeing with. Learn your lesson and move on to the next question. Any successful salesperson will tell you that this is true. Once you disentangle your self-esteem from other people's reaction to you, you are well on your way to getting what you really want.

I remember when I decided to get through my rejection quota. I had always felt I wasn't good enough. And I was addicted to rejection. It was my favorite way of torturing myself with the pain of my own inadequacy. Sometimes I'd try to kick the habit by not asking for what I wanted, thereby protecting myself from failure, but losing something valuable in the process.

One day in the fall of 1976 a friend suggested to me that perhaps I hadn't been rejected enough. This warped idea struck home. I began to think that I had this "rejection quota" I hadn't yet fulfilled, that when I got rejected enough I would come to see it was nothing personal and begin to accept myself more. In any case, the idea intrigued me and I decided to test it out by doing a little experiment. I would stand on Fifth Avenue and proposition every beautiful woman I saw until I got through my fear of rejection.

I remember the first attempt. This beautiful blonde approached—a real Farrah Fawcett. My body was shaking like an Osterizer, but I figured, what the hell, you gotta start sometime, so I shot out in front of her, stopping her in her tracks.

"Excuse me, Miss," I said, my voice faltering. We looked at each other and I could see every weird thought running through her mind. I mean I could literally see me from her eyes. "Are you busy tonight?" She laughed once, then again. Then she cleared her throat demurely and walked around me as if I were some piece of furniture in her way. I was crushed, totally devastated. I slithered to a storefront to gather the pieces. Tears streamed down my face. My body was practically convulsing. How interesting! A woman I don't know said no and I was a basket case!

Of course I was not to be defeated by one knockdown, no matter how humiliated I felt. I was determined to get up on my feet, summon all my strength and go the distance. I stood on that corner all day, and two days after. I must have approached 100 women—all knockouts, mind you. Some of them walked right over me. Others gave me a few jabs, the Ali shuffle, then danced away. A few, not many—well, one—I had against the ropes, but then her husband appeared.

It was funny, though, After the first seventy or so, it began to feel different. I mean, at first, each time I'd get a no, it felt like the end of the world. But after a while it didn't hurt so much. Maybe I was expecting the worst so there was less disappointment, but I think it was more than that.

All these women saying no to me—I could see that they were really saying yes. I mean, I was the one saying no. I was saying "Bob, you're no good. The women you want always reject you." These were my thoughts about myself. These women weren't rejecting me. They were, in some weird way, agreeing with my judgments about myself. It got to the point where one said no, and I felt nothing in my body—I mean, nothing negative. I smiled and thanked her and really meant it. I could see and feel the utter perfection of that no.

★ *The fear of success is far greater than the fear of failure.*

When they said yes, a new kind of terror gripped me—the fear of actually receiving what I had always kept out of my life. I learned that the fear of failure, as horrible as it is, is actually safer than the fear of success. Perhaps we are accustomed to failure, sacrifice and compromise. It is familiar to us. We know we can survive it. Success, however, is unknown, uncharted territory. I remember the first time I received a large sum of money in my life. Someone was handing me the check, and my hand was sweating, my body trembling and my heart throbbing like I was in mortal danger. "Can I really have this?" I was thinking. "Will this lead to some horrible punishment? Am I good enough? What will my parents think?" I remembered, while holding the check and crying, my mother telling me that she was only living to see me be a success. "Will she die now?" I wondered. "Oh, God! Can I really handle this?" A vision of suicide flashed by me.

Success is the greatest challenge to your life urge!

People react to us the way we react to ourselves. Let's face it: Often we are more comfortable with rejection than acceptance. It's more familiar, an old friend we can depend on. To be accepted is to receive more loving energy than we are accustomed to handling. It can make us squirm and twitch. That feeling of overwhelm, of sinking into quicksand, can quickly pass through us.

The lesson of "unrequited" love is a valuable one once you let yourself get it. If you fall in love with someone who doesn't feel the same way, you have an opportunity to learn how to give love freely, without expectation of anything in return. Loving without strings attached is loving unconditionally. You can free yourself of the neediness, dependency and loneliness you still have associated with love when someone seems to reject you.

Rejection is an opportunity to love yourself more fully.

All rejection supports you in accepting yourself more fully.

On the other hand, when someone falls in love with you and you don't feel the same way, you have a chance to receive love without feeling obligated. You can tell this person exactly how you feel, allow him or her to feel as he or she does, and relax. Love doesn't always have to mean something significant.

Love doesn't indebt you to someone. Receiving love freely gives the giver the pleasure of knowing his love is good enough and has reached its target.

Saying yes when you mean yes and no when you mean no creates greater joy in your heart and clarity in your relationships.

Mastering the giving part of receiving and the receiving part of giving restores integrity to your heart, overcoming the need to keep score on your relationship.

Self-love is a redundant expression because, in a sense, the self is love. Self-love is simply the experience of oneself without anything in the way.

If you were to experience yourself without any judgments, reservations or considerations, you would naturally like yourself. If you were to stop comparing yourself to others and experience yourself for what you are, you would naturally like yourself. If you were to stop trying to please others in the hope that their approval would make you all right with yourself, you would naturally like yourself.

It's perfectly natural to like oneself!

Self-love is not egotism. An egotist hates himself but acts as though he's God's gift to the universe. An egotist is a phony. He shows off, brags and pretends to be what he fears he isn't. Since no amount of effort can overcome a basis repugnance for oneself, egotism is an expression of futility. The thought is, if only I can trick others into loving me, maybe I can gain a moment's respite from hating myself. Unfortunately, positive reinforcement means nothing when you've written yourself off.

Since people tend to confirm the opinions you have of yourself, if you're walking around thinking "I'm no good, I'm no good, I'm no good," you will automatically attract friends, co-workers, bosses and lovers who put you down. If your basic evaluation of yourself is "I'm no good," if that's a Primal Law that governs you, when someone says you're no good you will secretly gloat (even as you sulk). You will feel strangely vindicated. You'll know you were right all along. Your worst suspicion about yourself will be confirmed, and a part of you will be relieved. On the other hand, if people come along and tell you you're the greatest, your pattern of invalidation will have a field day. "Bullshit!" you'll think. Either they're lying in order to make me feel better, or else they're not so hot themselves. Certainly not very perceptive. If your mind accepted their acknowledgment, you'd have to make yourself wrong. And you know you're right! You're no good. Your whole life is living proof of your worthlessness.

On the other hand, if you value yourself, you will tend to attract others who support your opinion. Only two people who love themselves unconditionally are in a position to begin loving each other.

The more you love yourself, the more love you have to share with others!

I teach prosperity seminars, and I always ask my students "How much are you worth to yourself?" The question stuns many of them. It's such a point-blank way of connecting love and money, the two areas where many of us feel a lack. What are you worth to yourself? How can the work you do or the item you sell have value if you, the worker, don't value yourself?

Many of us were brought up with the idea that it's better to be self-less than self-ish, better to be self-effacing than self-assertive. Self-denial, while often valuable as a discipline for purification, can become dangerous if it turns into an obsession based on the thought that there is something wrong with you.

Self-deprivation based on guilt is punishment, no matter how cleverly disguised!

The truth is, all service begins with the self and all service is self-serving. If you have a passion for helping mankind, you will be effective to the extent that you feel you have something valuable to offer to the planet. It is only by nourishing the self—and nothing is as nourishing as unconditional love—that we have the capacity to serve others. Service based on high self-esteem is doubly rewarding, as it contributes to the well-being of others and at the same time replenishes that reservoir of love within you. If you deny yourself love, you will descend into the depth of martyrdom, giving and sacrificing until there is nothing left to give. How exhausting!

Be clear on what you really want in your life. Many people complain about not getting what they want, but if you ask them what they do want, the response is "I don't know." Not defining your goals is a clear invitation for your subconscious mind to manifest at will. *Much of what we call "flowing with it" is an excuse for not taking the responsibility to ask for what we want.*

If you take the responsibility for the creation of your life and clear out your negative attitudes you will manifest your true desires in life.

It's important to say no to what you don't want in life, as well as to individuals. So many of us have the habit of compromise. We repeatedly say yes to what we don't want and then we wonder why things don't go our way. You'll take a job you don't really want, thinking nothing better will come along, or you'll get into a relationship you know is not your true desire, thinking it's better than nothing, and then years later find yourself feeling trapped by compromises, full of regret and bitterness.

★ *Saying no to what you don't want opens the space to receive what you do want.*

Often people create jealousy because they don't have enough self-esteem to ask for what they really want. Perhaps you agree to an "open" form of sexual relationship because you are afraid of losing your partner entirely if you don't. Your thought is "I'd rather have half of him than be alone!" If you knew you deserved someone's exclusive devotion, you could never be thinking along these lines. To love your partner more than you love yourself is a true crime of the heart.

So you create the upset called jealousy in order to learn your basic self-esteem lesson: "You deserve all the love you desire!"

Jealousy is watching someone from whom you think you need attention give it to someone or something else.

Jealousy is watching someone from whom you think you need attention give it to someone or something else. It is also a socially acceptable way for feeling a lot of primal feelings which don't ordinarily surface. As such it is a powerful healing opportunity. (In some places a "crime of passion" is even pardonable.)

There are two primary thoughts at the root of jealousy: "The source of love is outside of me" and "There is a scarcity of love."

If the source of love is your mate and there is not enough to go around, observing your mate loving someone else, however innocently, can throw you into primal panic—a life-or-death crisis in which you relive the separation anxiety of cutting the umbilical cord.

Jealousy contains every emotion. It takes you completely out of present time into the murky realm of dark, subliminal memories and future fear fantasies. Jealousy is the best emotional roller coaster in town!

There are things you can do when seized by a jealous fit. First, do not disapprove of yourself for it. People are so embarrassed by their jealousy that they often lie about it and use it to lower their self-esteem instead of raise it. Let your jealousy be! Work on the self-esteem implants at the end of this chapter. Get rebirthed. If you've agreed to let your partner be with someone or something else (you can be jealous of his work, card game or golf game) do not sulk and feel sorry for yourself. Remember, you are the source of, and have the power to create, alternative forms of pleasure and love in your life. If your rage swells up, pound pillows, throw bottles against a wall, find a "creative blame" surrogate. If you have to cry, cry!

Also, take a good look at what part of your mind created the situation—so you don't have to repeat it. Is it a childhood pattern of sibling rivalry because you and your sister competed for dad's exclusive attention? Are you acting out your fear of loss in order to release the pain of your parents' divorce? Or maybe it's your addiction to triangles, a clear sign of suppressed or unresolved incestuous feelings.

By *incestuous* I refer to the part of you that thinks you have to come between people in order to get the love you want. Often in childhood, even in the womb, our parents experience some separation in their relationship around our presence. This is a result of their thinking, of course, but out of your love for them you might have taken on the guilt. Since guilt causes you to repeat what you are guilty of until you work it out, you might subconsciously be pushing your mate away because you don't feel you deserve to be closer to him than your parents were to each other. Your thought might be "My love causes separation; therefore I don't deserve love!" It is difficult to bond completely with a mate if you are still addicted to triangular guilt. The more intimate you become with someone, the more you will secretly want to sabotage the relationship.

I remember times when my partner was jealous and I refused to take any responsibility for it. "It's her problem," I'd think, "her insecurity, her low self-esteem." This was at a time in my life when I only took 50 percent responsibility for my relationships, not 100 percent. But as these jealous situations kept recurring, I had to admit—much as my ego hated to—there was some unknown consciousness factor in me contributing to these upsets. I did a self-interrogation: "The reason I want my partner to be jealous is . . . ." and I was amazed by what I discovered. In my mind a woman didn't love me completely unless she was possessive and jealous. I remembered my mother reading my love letters and eavesdropping on the phone when I was a teenager. In my mind a woman had to act like my mother if she really loved me. Just seeing this pattern did a whole lot to clarify and eventually eliminate most jealousy from my life.

It doesn't matter whether it is you or your mate who feels jealous. You both create the upset.

When your partner is jealous, it can be a powerful reminder to you of your priorities. Perhaps your ship is off course. Perhaps you're "running" a leaving pattern, a revenge pattern or an incest pattern. Your partner's jealousy can be the jolt you need to move from unconscious behavior to conscious choice.

☆ *Jealousy is a wonderful (if crazy) opportunity for both partners to raise their self-esteem and get clear about what they want.* You deserve the full attention of your partner. If your partner doesn't want to give you what you want, you may have to choose between your addiction to a painful pattern and the relationship you really want. *Remember, you never lose anything that supports your highest good.*

You never lose anything that's for your highest good.

The higher your self-esteem, the more you are empowered to choose for your highest good!

If you feel lonely or empty at the core, clinging to a loving person will not dissolve those feelings, though you may find temporary comfort. The way through loneliness is by yourself—alone. Only you can cut the cords, bury the past and reclaim your personal power. Only you can say goodbye!

When being alone becomes more of a gift than a torture, you know you don't need anyone to make you happy. Then you can choose relationships that automatically reflect the love you've found within.

You deserve yourself! Begin to think: "I am now the person I always wanted to be like!"

Implants to Raise Your Self-Esteem

I love myself no matter what!

I love myself in the presence of others.

My presence is naturally pleasing to myself and others.

I am now the person I always wanted to be like!

I approve of my life!

I love my life!

I deserve the very best in life!

I love myself for asking for what I want, regardless of the response.

I love myself when people say no to me.

It's safe to surpass my parents.

I can surpass my parents and not lose their love.

The truth is, my parents want the best for me too.

I am willing to be successful, even if it means pleasing my parents.

I forgive myself for failing in order to make my parents wrong.

It's safe to surpass myself!

People want me to have what I want.

The more I have what I want, the more others have what they want.

I have the power to succeed.

Just because I misused my power in the past doesn't mean I can't use it right now!

I trust myself!

I trust my intuition.

I am a good person; I deserve the good life!

Chapter X

No more hiding from God

Iwas once a proud atheist, then an agnostic because that felt even more special. I was a rebel, rejecting my religious background. God is used to justify so many contradictory points of view that I decided if God did exist He must be a fairly wishy-washy fellow at best and a complete hypocrite at worst. I noticed that people used the concept of God to justify their personal notions of right and wrong, good and bad, and I wondered if God had any existence at all apart from religion. Finally I figured out that if God did exist, He seemed to manifest His presence as absence. God loved to play hide-and-seek. Didn't He have anything better to do?

The more I came to know life, the less I seemed to understand it. There was no way I could fit my peak experiences, which were gradually growing in quantity and quality, into the neat little pigeon holes of my Aristotelean mind. Every once in a while my mind would turn to God again, but pictures of religious wars, the Spanish Inquisition and the Salem witch trials would distract me. I'd think of the movie *The Ten Commandments* and God would seem very hard and demanding, like mountain climbing.

Then I had a series of experiences that opened me up to a God I never knew, and I came to see that God was not the One who had been hiding, I was. One such experience occurred in the middle of Death Valley the first time I traveled outside New York. I was so amazed by the tremendous space surrounding me that all I could do was lie on the desert floor, sandwiched between the earth and the firmament, breathing uncontrollably. I literally forgot who I was; all that space outside of me began to feel as if it were inside me. I was sure someone had turned me inside out.

Another time, I was rebirthing when suddenly a voice called out to me "I am here!" It might have been my rebirther or it might have been my next-door neighbor, but I knew it was God!

What is God? Is He the force, the source, nature, an old man with a beard who sits on a throne in the sky, a woman, some cosmic god-father, or the opiate of the people? Who is this masked man?

God for me is the most personal of all concepts and I would not presume to impose my notion of God on you. But I do know that opening your heart to the God of your imagination can open the door to everything. So I would like to share with you the God I have come to know.

I recently read a science magazine which described a conference of top religious and scientific leaders. Their goal was to define a God for the twenty-first century; it would be a God grounded in common sense, humanity and scientific likelihood. After much debate they concluded that God was "universe": a unifying energy principle at work at all times and places.

For me God is that sense of everything making sense, that justice beyond all apparent injustice, that purposeful force driving the universe forward. God is the Infinite, the part of us that transcends our limited sense of who we are, the Spirit-self into which we can surrender and experience a perfect spiritual connection and correlation between our inner life and external reality. God is the intuitive knowledge that we are one, that all of creation are as cells of one organism working separately and at the same time together. In God we are a Divine chain gang.

God is the stars and the space between.

God is everyone and everything and, at the same time, no one and nothing. God is invisible and always in plain sight. God is creation and destruction, war and peace, the stars and the space between, the USA and USSR, peanut butter and jelly. God is the mystery of science and the science of mystery.

Since God is the unknown, the more you know you don't know, the closer you are to God!

Since God is the Infinite, to the extent that you feel separate from God you tend to feel helpless, powerless and limited. Opening your heart entails touching a presence larger than you!

If not God, who?

Everything there is to say about God has been said many times, yet the truth about God remains unspeakable.

In most relationships people stay stuck in their ego-cells, as shown in the diagram. As they are drawn together, they feel the love between them (that wants to experience union) and their minds' addiction to separation.

The ego cannot surrender. The very premise of its existence is separation, and love is its greatest threat. So the closer you get to someone, the more your heart says "Let go" and your mind says "Hold on for dear life."

God

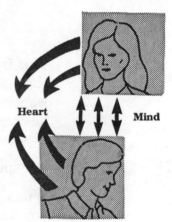

Heart   Mind

Clear yourself of all your thoughts about God. At the top of a piece of paper write, "God..." and free-associate all your thoughts about God. On another piece of paper, write "My father is..." and fill up that page. On a third page, do the same for your mother. Notice how many of your thoughts about God are extensions of your parents, the major authorities of your childhood. Circle the thoughts about God that you want to retain, adding others, crossing out the rest.

This is why in many loving relationships people start fighting when they get intimate. The conflict is actually the result of the love wanting to push you through the wall of separation that your ego has constructed. But no amount of struggle can overcome a thought of separation. It must be released.

The union love desires results from a leap of faith.

When your desire to surrender is greater than your fear of loss, then you know God. Then you and your partner can meet in God and form a holy triangle: a relationship that seeks to share its experience of love without separation in the world. Imagine if the whole world would overcome separation and join in a higher, holy purpose. We'd be a planet of Jedi knights.

Sometimes when people get enlightened, they become intoxicated by the power of their own minds. They are seduced by the concept of being the source, at cause of all their existence.

Make no mistake about it—this is the seduction of the ego, wanting you to think that your mind is God and your spirit is not. The ego is God's envious kid brother. It wants to be God. It wants to control and manipulate and play chess with the universe.

But, alas, all the ego can create is illusion, the illusion of power, the illusion of love, the illusion of happiness. The ego can only create what is not. God has already created all that is!

If you become trapped in your ego, it is easy to tell. Your ego will try to convince you that you are more spiritual than others, that only you know the real God, that the physical universe is beneath you.

The physical universe is just as much God as anything else, for one of the primary aspects of God is that He cannot separate Himself from Himself.

God does not know separation. He is inseparable from His Creation!

(It is probable that, at birth, when the cord is cut and we are "split" from our mothers, we decide we are separate. The pain of our first delivery, our infant guilt and Primal Law, cause us to conclude on some level that God has cast us out of his Kingdom. In this sense, every birth recapitulates the story of the Garden of Eden: Leaving the womb becomes a punishment for some hideous unknown crime we have committed. And the trauma of our first delivery makes spiritual deliverance a frightening proposition to many of us.)

To the extent that you are connected to God, you know that everything outside yourself also resides within, and you experience this connection. The physical universe is clearly the mirror of your spiritual evolution.

One of the keys to God is to see everyone as God, whether or not they conform to your mind's pictures of God.

I used to think that people who prayed were like children who would go to Macy's every December, sit on the lap of Santa Claus, and tell him what they wanted for Christmas. This was all very well, but when it came down to it, mom and dad had to stand at the cashier and pay for everything.

Then I heard that "God helps those who help themselves" and that seemed to make sense. God is obviously in the self-improvement business.

Now prayer makes perfect sense to me. To pray is simply to implant high-quality thoughts in your subconscious mind and to have faith that your thought is law in God's universe.

As Emily Dickinson put it:

> *A word*
> *is dead*
> *when it*
> *is said,*
> *some say;*
> *I say*
> *it just*
> *begins*
> *to live*
> *that day.*

Your prayers are God's living words in the universe. You do not want to pray to some "pie-in-the-sky" deity who may or may not listen to you. You pray to the God within, to your spirit-self.

Whenever you create you create in association with God. You are, after all created in the image of God, the Creator!

Creation in any form is a holy act!

Learn how to listen to your God. Close your eyes, take a deep breath and let it go. Ask God if He is there. Listen to your heart, not your mind. Even if your mind protests "Who are you to talk to God?" "Have you gone nuts?", persist!

To hear God is to hear the voice of your intuition. You can begin to talk to God without thinking you are crazy. The fear of insanity is usually based on both the fear of surrender and the fear of disapproval. Your self-esteem is now high enough to let God into your life anew, no matter what anyone thinks.

Every night before going to bed, take out a piece of paper and make a list of "Something I'm grateful for, something I forgive myself for and something I pray for." If you do this on a regular basis, you will soon notice your prayers turning into gratitudes.

God is your personal prerogative!

When you have a problem, it's fine to ask God to correct your misperceptions on the subject. You can turn impossible situations over to Him. For God, the impossible is ordinary.

Many people miss God completely because they look for extraordinary signs or miracles. The truth is: God is always giving you miracles, only they are so ordinary you take them for granted. A bird, a flower, an ocean, a child—is there any lack of miracles to testify to God's presence?

The more you handle what's working in your life, the more God handles the rest. That is not to say that you should sit back, babble to God all day and await further miracles. You do have free will. Your choices do have consequences in the real world. But the more you connect with the particular gifts and talents you possess and the more willing you are to share them, the more of a contribution you make to the evolution of quality on the planet. That is how God's will gets done!

Sometimes people erroneously think that surrendering to the Oneness means losing their individual identities. Not so. Surrendering to God is tapping your individual creativity far more than the ego can provide for you.

Often we secretly resent God for giving us free will. Much as we value our freedom, sometimes it seems like life would be easier if some benign Father ran the whole show. If there were a God, this reasoning goes, He would make sure we chose correctly all the time.

Freedom is the experience of choosing.

Well, you'll just have to forgive God for giving you the freedom you probably value next to life itself.

The more you love your life, the more you come to appreciate what an incredible job God has done. And the more you live your life in the realm of loving thoughts, words and deeds, the more you begin to see the possibilities for heaven on earth.

Stop hiding from God.

Certainly, at the very least, God deserves a second chance!

Implants on God

God has already forgiven me.

The divine plan of my life is now manifesting.

I now trust God.

Since God is the unknown, the more I know I don't know, the closer I am to God.

I am now willing for God to correct all my misperceptions.

I forgive God for creating me with free will.

The more I handle what's working in my life, the more God takes care of the rest.

Thank God for me!

God is my constant companion!

God is now with me!

God is with me no matter what I think or feel!

Even when I don't feel God's presence, God is with me!

It's OK to talk to God.

God gives me permission to be myself.

My connection to God is now good enough for me to accomplish what I want in life.

God's will be done!

God bless the planet Earth!

Chapter XI

The Master Key

Iremember going to Montreal several years ago. Sondra Ray (founder of the Loving Relationships Training) and I were about to lead our first Montreal training. No sooner had we arrived than a local newspaper caught our eyes. On the front page a headline read "The First 106 Years Are a Snap!" What followed was the story of a remarkable man.

Being immortalists, we decided to visit this ancient being. We arrived at a nursing home, where our "friend" was under observation, half expecting to find a withered-up shell of a man. What we found was anything but: Here was a man who was all heart!

He was a diminutive being, brimming with unbridled life. His eyes twinkled and his ears were long and pointed, like Spock's. Why he was in a nursing home was beyond us—or him. He was ready to run around the block! The doctors wanted to examine him on his birthday, however, because they figured if he was that old there surely must be something wrong with him! Not so. He was in A-1 condition.

His daughter, 77, sat by his side. She looked dreadful, ready for her death bed. We asked her what her problem was and she told us she was exhausted from trying to keep up with her father. In her mind, his aliveness was killing her.

Then we turned our attention to this little old dynamo. What was the secret to his longevity? Had he bathed in the Fountain of Youth? Was he really an alien from a planet of immortalists? My mind was working overtime trying to figure this guy out.

He began to describe his childhood in a small Latvian town: how strangers were welcome into everyone's home, how even beggars were invited in for fine meals. The feeling of family animating this man was overwhelming. Tears streamed down his face as he talked.

He told us of his love for Canada. His passion for the people exploded in his bellowing voice and in his fist, clenched to emphasize his feelings. I was almost envious of the amount of life his little body contained.

He was a revolutionary of sorts, but far beyond politics. Here was a man totally in love with life, with human beings, with family. Here was a man whose heart was so open it seemed to embrace the whole planet. This man and his daughter were living proof that youth is a function of the mind, that the body ages only after the mind and heart lose faith.

This man was a distinct exception to the general rule: Most people die according to family tradition, usually within five years of the family member they most identified with. This is not a secret, it's common knowledge. Also, many people die shortly after retirement, when they feel their purpose in life is complete, or when their children get married, have children and become successful. Whenever the particular thought they've been living for is manifested, their reason for living is over. Insurance companies make billions of dollars by correctly predicting when people will die.

How does it feel to know that your death is a safe bet?

The thought that death is inevitable is just a thought, however popular, and however much collective substance it has behind it. Whether the thought is true or not, you might want to examine the practical ramifications of embracing a deathist philosophy—the despair, depression, scarcity, hopelessness, sickness and panic that death evokes. The belief in death, together with your Primal Law, comprise the ego's stranglehold on your life. Death is to the ego what life is to God; as long as you are tied down by death, it is impossible to take that leap of faith into spiritual life. That is why every such leap can be described as a living-death experience. Whenever you surrender into God, your ego dies, proving the illusory quality of death.

Unfortunately, whenever you return to doubt, your ego is resurrected with a new bag of tricks.

The thought of death is, ultimately, the thought that you are separate from God, that you are in fact guilty, and that your punishment is a life sentence. It is the belief that you have been cast out of Eden for your sins and that you must suffer through the birth/death cycle as a consequence.

The belief in a killer God is the ego's last laugh and is best summed up in this Elizabethan quote: "As flies to wanton boys are we to the gods; they kill us for their sport!" How absurd!

Every spiritual belief system must contend with the issue of death, because the more you release all your negative programming, the more the energy that previously surrounded it gravitates towards your Number One limiting program—the inevitability of death.

Your unconscious death urge is frequently activated when you are on the verge of spiritual breakthrough. Your plants start to die, your pet gets ill, your car breaks down or your teeth decay. This is the physical universe reflecting your belief in death and your ego seducing you into utter hopelessness. You might as well give up your quest and settle for compromise like everyone else.

Often when one of your parents dies or you reach the age of their deaths, your death urge will erupt. Your finances might collapse, your marriage fall apart, or your hair fall out.

Obviously, the more pain and discomfort you create in your physical body, the more tempting death will seem as an alternative. Why go on? What's the point? Nothing matters anyway! Most old people who choose to die do so for this reason. They are letting go of the pain the only way they know how. And far be it from me to make them wrong. Death is clearly a viable and valid choice when you reach the point of no return, though the message here is that it is not necessarily inevitable that you reach that point.

Other indications of an active death urge are the feeling that time is running out, your days are numbered, you're living on borrowed time and you're a prisoner of time.

Isn't it ironic that, on the one hand, we believe that time heals all wounds and, on the other hand, we consider the sands of time running through the hour glass of our lives?

Your life urge is stronger than your death urge!

The more you love your life, however, the more you will want more of it, and the more you will discover ways to create more of it. An open heart always touches the infinite, and the infinite is a source of endless inspiration.

Become conscious of your family tradition of death. Draw a family tree, going back three generations. List all your major relatives and ancestors, the dates of their births and deaths and the causes. See if you can locate any patterns you want to release.

If you're living on borrowed time, it is important to remember that you took out the loan in the first place and that therefore your credit must be good. In other words, death is an agreement you made which you might want to renegotiate. Perhaps your grandfather, whom you loved, died peacefully in his sleep at 80 and you said to yourself "That's the way I want to go." You may not have thought about it for many years, but that thought is like a time bomb in your body.

☆ *You must choose death before death can choose you!*

Children have an incredibly difficult time grasping the concept of death, which indicates, at least to me, that something is off. This is partly due to all the lies, myths and double messages we receive about death as kids. Parents are more flustered talking to their children about death than they are about sex. Also, as children we have an intuitive sense of immortality, perhaps because we are more psychically sensitive, our hearts not having succumbed to social pressure yet. As children we tend to feel that death is a story grownups made up.

The following is a real story from a real newspaper which shows just how immortal children can be.

Baby Run Over by Dozer Survives

Green Cove Springs, FL (AP) An 18-month-old boy survived virtually unscathed despite being run over by his father's bulldozer, and doctors and sheriff's officals say they can't explain how he survived.

Dewey McCall's father, Melvin, was driving the bulldozer last week when it suddenly slipped out of gear, jerking McCall and sending the toddler sprawling. To his horror, McCall looked down and saw the child's legs jutting from the tractor tread, three tons of metal pinning the tiny body into the hard-packed earth.

But Dewey wasn't dead.

He was rushed to the hospital, where X-rays revealed no broken bones and no internal damage.

On Friday he was released from Clay Memorial Hospital.

"I have absolutely no explanation of how that child survived," said Lt. Derry Dedmon of the Clay County Sheriff's Office, who investigated the incident. "We couldn't even get our hands under the tread."

Dedmon said the only evidence of Dewey's ordeal were a few tread marks on his back and a cut on his head.

"It was just a real freak occurrence," said hospital administrator Steven Hitt, who said doctors had no medical explanation for the child's survival.

About three feet of tread had run over the child. McCall slowly rolled the bulldozer off Dewey's body, which made a dent in the ground.

"His little eyes bulged out . . . He looked so flat. He just looked like he was spread out all over the ground," McCall said.

Dewey regained consciousness as they rushed him to the hospital, his whine building into a steady wail. After shocked doctors completed their examination, they kept him for two days for observation.

The more you hear stories like Dewey's, the more you remember when you felt you were invulnerable, when you dared to live life fully and take chances you would never consider taking now.

Of course, your ego wants you to believe that death is real and inevitable, because as long as you do there is no chance of escaping from its closed system. And the more love you receive, the more your unconscious death urge is aroused. Most murders are committed in families.

Love and death are incompatible partners. You surely want to divorce your heart from the fear of death. When you do, your heart can once again take the risks it never hesitated about as a child.

When you meet someone and recognize the love between you, that love is eternal, you are experiencing an eternal connection, an awakening beyond time and space. How else can you explain feeling so deeply toward someone you never "knew" before. On some level, you must be remembering something you didn't realize you knew.

Love is not measurable. It is not a commodity to be possessed in time and space. Only an open heart can possess love! If you try to hold onto it, it will slip away until you have nothing. Hoarding love is like hoarding money. The more you receive, the more you feel you'll never have enough. It is only by letting love go that love flows freely through you.

Love is the eternal stream of life itself!

That is why the concept of strangers is so absurd. What determines when a stranger becomes a friend? How many cups of coffee, conversations or dates does it take? In fact, you know a whole lot about people when you first meet them. If your heart is open, you receive a wealth of intuitive and telepathic information on first sight.

A stranger is someone with whom you feel strange.

There are no strangers. We are one world family in the process of self-recognition. *A stranger is just someone you feel strange with.* The more comfortable you are with yourself in the presence of people, the more strangers seem like old friends.

How can you surrender to this wisdom in your heart, much less commit yourself to everlasting loving relationships, if you are not safe in the physical universe? (And you are not safe so long as death is lurking in the corners of your unconscious mind.) How can you let go of the control and feel the full power and joy of love if, subconsciously, you fear your well might run dry?

Whenever you seem to lose something of value, it's only to make room for something better.

How can you surrender to the immortality of love when you think the more you use your energy, the more depleted you become? You suffer from a lifelong energy crisis, carefully saving your emotional and physical resources, for fear you'll run out of life prematurely.

Many people experience this fear most intensely while making love. The more excited they get, the more they subconsciously hold on. The more pleasure and aliveness they feel, the more they hold their breath. The fear of a heart attack is often greatest during sex. (Sex and death have always been associated. The French call orgasm *le petit mort;* The metaphysical poets referred to climax as death.)

Make *a list of ten ways to increase your pleasure and aliveness. Schedule them into your calendar on a regular basis.*

Mortal relationships are a dead-end street—at best a temporary escape from inevitable doom. Either you choose to die together or else you make a U-turn and head out on the treacherous freeway of life again. Some choice!

If your relationships are grounded in your unconscious death urge, your priorities get twisted. Security replaces safety as a major concern. You begin to think that if you acquire enough material goods, you can ward off the evils of the cold, cruel world. You succumb to the Howard Hughes Syndrome, your basic paranoia causing you to construct more elaborate defense systems the richer you get. The quality of your life is reduced to survival in the jungle. You forget that you know how to survive and that what matters now is how, not whether, you'll make it.

Your body is the closest part of the physical universe to you.

Your body is the closest part of the physical universe to you, yet how much responsibility do you take for it? Most people know more about fixing their cars than healing their bodies, let alone youthing them. Doctors make millions of dollars from people's helplessness about their own bodies. What a racket!

Immortality Consciousness	Survival Consciousness
Love	Separation
Abundance	Scarcity
Health	Disease
Peace	Conflict
Ease	Struggle
Pleasure	Pain
Joy	Depression
Satisfaction	Frustration
Safety	Security
Success	Failure
Intimacy	Withholding
God	Rebellion
Innocence	Guilt
Aliveness	Suppression
Surrender	Resistance
Intuition	Understanding

Your body is a friend, not a stranger. It continually communicates a wide range of messages concerning your subconscious mind. If your back hurts, you're not getting the support you need; if your legs hurt, you fear moving ahead; if your shoulders ache, you're carrying too much of a burden. Your eyes? What don't you want to see?

You can begin to heal your body of minor aches and pains right now if you are willing to interrogate it, locate the root causes in your subconscious mind, uproot them and implant new loving thoughts. At the same time you should take full advantage of the best medical advice you can get, especially when the ailment seems serious and beyond the limits of your own healing powers at present. The point is not to invalidate Western medicine, but to encourage you to establish a loving relationship with your body and to take responsibility for what goes on within it.

Disease is, first of all, a lack of ease; it is a clear sign that you need to relax and take it easy for awhile. Begin to see all sickness as a collection of physical symptoms being released. Often these symptoms are the healing-in-progress, but because you believe so firmly in the idea of sickness (perhaps as a subconscious way of playing weak and helpless and getting the emotional support you don't ordinarily give yourself) you unwittingly inhibit the complete release. Also, we are a culture addicted to temporary relief as opposed to permanent healing. We all too readily anesthetize our unpleasant symptoms with pain killers, but more than the pain dies in the process.

Notice your physical, as well as mental, addictions. What, in your mind, does it take for you to survive? Three square meals and eight hours of sleep per night? Or perhaps it's no meat, brown rice and organic vegetables? We are creatures of habit, and most of our habits are reflections of either unconscious or conscious survival belief systems. Usually we either conform to or rebel from our family's beliefs in health. In either case, whether you are a meat-and-potatoes person or a whole-grain person, you are probably at the effect of food, sleep and shelter rather than at choice. You might want to begin to experiment with such addictions and release the feelings and thoughts that surface when you do so.

Nowadays we have a race of super-purists, people who believe not only in pollution but that everything they take into their bodies threatens to contaminate their precious bodily fluids. If your basic belief is in an impure universe out to get you, you can never purify your body and your environment enough to generate true safety. Nutritional and environmental paranoia are walls of the ego's fortress as much as more conventional fear thoughts.

An immortalist is one whose context in life is safety, not attack. If you embrace a value system based on the eternal, supportive qualities of life, rather than the mortal ones, you are at a psychological advantage to create greater health and aliveness in your body's ecology. You can begin to relax your body, let go of aging thoughts and practice youthing yourself. The fountain of youth is ultimately the infinite reservoir of love in your heart.

An open mind can open your heart and body to greater energy than you have ever known. A rigid body is the mirror of a rigid mind and heart.

Rigidity is fragility. Mental and emotional relaxation is the key to physical endurance, resiliency and longevity.

The paradox is this: An open mind and heart will surely open your body to spiritual replenishment, recharging the cells with new vitality and added years; but unless you begin by entertaining, if not embracing, the concept of immortality, you will not create a context to provide you with the safety you need to open up.

The choice is clear: "To be or not to be," whether it is wiser to focus on your life force and dwell in the kingdom of everlasting life, or to accept your mortality as an inevitable cliff from which you must descend and hover on the precipice of life, "suffering the slings and arrows of an outrageous fortune."

In relationships the choice for greater joy and aliveness forms the foundation for lasting commitment. If you and your mate, or you and a friend, are devoted to both your own and each other's ever-increasing well-being, commitment to expanding aliveness becomes the basis for an immortal loving relationship.

For most of my life I didn't know what true commitment was. I got it confused with agreements. Now I realize that agreements, while sometimes useful early in a relationship, come from the mind and in no way are a substitute for genuine commitment, which springs from the heart. (A lawyer once told me that all agreements are based on mistrust. You don't trust someone in your heart, so you must protect yourself by having a contract which forces him to keep his word!)

I used to think you make a commitment and then you're stuck with it or you break it. Not so. You discover your commitment on different levels, and each time you discover it, it deepens. It's like a tree. You plant it and nourish it. Over time its roots take hold. Storms and droughts test the will and purpose of the tree. Each time a test is passed, a sense of deepening conviction and greater permanence emerges. So it is with love. At first you just notice you're in it. You experience that exquisite feeling of eternal recognition and connection. That's the first level of commitment. Then you make a series of decisions: We'll live together, travel together, pool our money, work together—whatever form best seems to suit our purpose in being together.

Fairly soon your love, as the tree, undergoes its own trials and tribulations. And each time you weather a storm, whether it's competition, jealousy or financial insecurity, you notice a deepening of your commitment, a strengthening of your love, an increasing sense of your reason for being one. The roots take hold. But the better it gets, the more your sabotage patterns emerge. The ego detests perfection and will do anything in its power to undermine you. The fear of entrapment and abandonment can tear at a loving relationship like a tornado. (In fact it is the subconscious memory of entrapment in the womb that causes the boxed-in feeling, the no-exit terror in relationships.) But the more you and your partner focus on your will to live, the more the life urge of your love defeats the death urge and the more you will prevail.

I used to think that freedom was opposed to commitment. Now I know better. *What most of us call freedom is really suspended animation. Hovering above all the options and opportunities of life and choosing nothing is not freedom; it is paralysis. Freedom of choice is only experienced in the act of choosing. It is only when you plunge yourself totally into a choice, be it work or love or family, that you discover your true freedom and the door of everything.*

How can you take the plunge if you are still paralyzed by the fear of loss? More often than not, you hold yourself back from love, keep score on life, and wait to see how your relationships turn out before choosing them fully. But without the choice, what chance do you have? You're not even fully in the relationship so long as your mind is watching, observing, judging. We are a culture of emotional cripples, handicapped by our own lack of faith.

It is important to acknowledge the love you feel when you feel it. Usually when people first fall in love, they can't stop telling each other how much they love each other. Then, as time goes by, "I love you" becomes a weekly or monthly expression, instead of an everyday occurrence. Then the words disappear completely. The relationship goes on automatic and unconscious patterns take over.

The more you acknowledge the love you feel, the more love you will have to feel. Love never dies, but it can go underground for awhile if neglected. What you acknowledge grows before your very eyes!

Peace is my passion!

When your passion for peace, joy and aliveness in your intimate relationship becomes integrated on a cellular level, you naturally want to share that purpose in the world.

There is far too much negativism on the planet today. Turn on your TV, open a newspaper or read a magazine—everywhere you look, reports of gloom and prophecies of doom fill the air.

How can you overcome your Primal Law, let alone open your heart to immortality, when your vision of the world is clouded by intimations of Armageddon?

How can you have confidence in life when everywhere you look you see war, hunger and death?

How can you harness your talents and energies and make a real contribution to the quality of life on the planet, a need we all have in order to feel good about ourselves, when you think your effort will be futile because cataclysm is inevitable? Having an optimistic world view supports the opening of your heart!

Many people would argue that negative developments are facts, and that being "well-informed" can motivate us into affirmative action. My opinion is that when the forces of destruction are seen as insurmountable and irreversible it's hard enough to get out of bed in the morning, let alone think you can overcome the overwhelming odds and make a real difference. "What's the point?" becomes a valid and rhetorical question, and when enough people think that thought we have a real earth-shattering problem on our hands.

Cynicism has been called the last refuge of romantics. Romantics believe there is escape from a stark reality, and will even die to prove their devotion to love. The Romeo and Juliet Syndrome is based on a tragic vision of life where love rejects life and life rejects love. Cynics, on the other hand, believe that there is no escape from life or death, and that doom is inevitable so we might as well resign ourselves to the inescapable.

Optimism is the philosophy of love and life.

The context for love is optimism!

Optimism spurs you to make optimum use of your potential. The facts you learn about the world correspond to the views you hold of the world. We all find the statistics we need to prove that our point of view is right. Have the courage to believe in the forces of aliveness and evolution. Locate and release your own personal "death wish," those thoughts based on the concept that death is inevitable (thoughts like "It's hopeless," "I don't have enough time," "I can't make it," "This is killing me," "I've got to get out of here," "What difference does it make anyway?")

As we have seen, most of these thoughts are probably from birth, and even if recent research into life extension and life after death seems inconclusive, it behooves you to ground your heart energy in thoughts of life, not death. If the beliefs you hold to your heart are the results you get in life, holding the belief that death is inevitable to your heart can only cause you heartache and heart-decay. And I mean this quite literally.

If you believe life is finite, you will always hold a part of yourself back, conserving your energy for the future. You will avoid taking risks because you will not feel safe in the physical universe. And the moments you feel most alive will lead to either shutting down or total exhaustion. You will feel as though you were born with one tank of gas, as it were, so you have to measure your life sparingly, or else use it up foolishly. You will be stuck in indecision, paralysis will grip you at every crossroad, and your life will be tainted by urgency and desperation. You will live in constant fear of wasting your time and, at the same time, believe that life is after all a waste of time. You will agree with collective thoughts of gas shortages, water shortages, energy crises and financial scarcity. The economic reflection of a culture based on death are products with built-in obsolescence, fashions constantly going out of fashion, and pleasure-seekers racing for immediate gratification as if there were no tomorrow. Death is no way to live.

If you don't reclaim your own power to believe in life and love, you render yourself helpless and powerless and susceptible to the collective myths of decay, depression and destruction.

Either you think for yourself or else others tell you what to think, in which case you either believe them but resent them or reject them without making up your own mind. Remember, the make-up of your own mind is your own business. If you're forever "out to lunch," you miss the moveable feast that is your birthright.

We live in an unlimited universe, only an infinitesimal fraction of which is known. The universe is not running out of gas. It is continually transforming itself, bursting with unexpected new light, galaxy tumbling upon galaxy, infinite sands forever shifting—but hardly through an hour glass.

The universe is still in creation. Its birth is incomplete.

Why should we be any different? Let's open our hearts to a universe of infinite possibility. Life is only predictable because we have always thought of it in that light. The more we open our hearts to the unknown, the more mystery and awe take over our minds, driving boredom, depression and anxiety from our bodies. How much more exciting is the passion of an open heart and the dream of immortality than the cheap sensationalism of a death-worshipping society.

Who can say what the limits of consciousness are? The mysteries of outer space are dwarfed by the uncharted territory of inner space. Reports of masters who can move objects with psychic energy—and can even dematerialize, rematerialize and transmute their bodies—might seem untenable to the non-believer. That is only natural, since a non-believer must invalidate in order to hold onto his non-belief. Nonetheless, recent scientific studies in Russia and America suggest that there is, indeed, more to heaven and earth than Newtonian predictability.

Many of the great scientists—the Einsteins and the Huxleys—acknowledged the role of divine inspiration in their own discoveries and were in awe of the unknown the more they came to know. Once you think you know it all, you've succumbed to the greatest ignorance of all, closing your heart to the spirit that gives you life and closing your imagination to the dreams that generate miracles.

Science fiction is rapidly becoming modern technology. Who can say with certainty that man will not one day learn to harness the power of his mind, body and spirit and participate consciously in his own journey towards perfection, which even Darwin's theory of natural selection implies. Who can say that we are not on the verge of playing an active role in the transformation of our own bodies. It is conceivable to me that there is an age dawning wherein man discards the entire birth/death cycle as an obsolete belief system—a vestigal organ from a bygone day.

Open your mind to unlimited possibility and abundance will fill your life!

Imagine an alien spaceship streaming towards planet Earth. Inside is a family of friendly intergalactic beings on an exploratory mission. What would they see? What would they say?

From such a perspective, who are we, we earthlings? Are we not one family of human beings minding the corner grocery store of our galaxy?

Earth is a family business.

Earth is a family business!

We squabble, we feud, we pretend to be separated by race, sex or nationality, by color or religion. We compete, we disapprove, we even threaten to blow ourselves up. But we are one family nonetheless!

The drama of unresolved family feelings, frictions and frustrations is perpetually projected on a planetary scale.

All healing begins at home. The vision of open heart therapy is the context of Earth as home.

Immortality is the master key: It opens the door to everything.

What is needed is an army of open heart homemakers, willing to heal their family relationships and then to crusade for practical loving based on mutual co-operation, caring and cultivating the best of every human being.

Immortalists naturally take greater responsibility for the world they live in. Their feeling is that since they plan on being here in some form forever, they want to be certain they live on a planet worth calling home.

Planetary consciousness results from opening your heart to the eternality of universe and noticing that Earth is our home base in the eternal scheme of things.

Immortalists also know that loving relationships never end, much as they may change form. The eternal recognition is eternal. The seeds of love we exchange with family, friends, co-workers and lovers are seeds of life. You can always find that love for someone, no matter how far away he is or how long ago you knew him.

Write *letters of completion to your mom and dad (whether they are alive or dead), to siblings and any ex-lovers or friends you need to communicate with. Let them be love letters, releasing the past, taking responsibility for old wounds, and affirming the eternal bond between you.*

Completion is a great place to start!

Completion is a great place to start!

Completion is the end of separation and the beginning of union.

Completion is the acknowledgment of perfection in the middle of imperfection.

Completion is the overcoming of ego and the triumph of spirit.

Completion is the willingness to forgive and be grateful, to let go of all the little loose ends you've been clinging to for fear that if you released them the void would be unbearable.

Completion is the recognition that loss is an illusion and that when we cut cords, we are liberated, not abandoned. We are free to experience union.

The more we release the buried wounds of yesterday, the more we open our hearts to the sunken treasures of tomorrow.

And today is a good day to start!

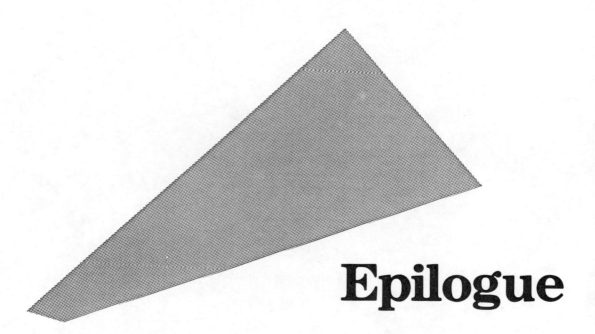

Epilogue

Friendship Is the Heart of Relationships

Good relationships are always grounded in friendship. What is a friend? A friend is someone on your team, someone you can trust, someone who knows your strengths and shortcomings and loves you unconditionally, someone who has compassion for your problems and supports your growth. A friend is, most of all, someone who likes as well as loves you and whom you like as well as love.

As mentioned previously, it does not necessarily take a long time to become friends with someone. It depends how long you want to wait before you let your guard down.

So often a loving relationship will be based on sex and a business relationship on money, or the other way around. Sometimes a relationship is based on helplessness, struggle, disapproval, revenge or incest. If your relationships originate in the spirit of friendship, it is far easier to resolve conflicts than it is to evolve a friendship from a conflicted relationship.

If you place friendship first, then your relationships don't end when they change form. Besides, it's doubly rewarding to be in love with a friend or do business with a friend.

Check Your Priorities

I used to have a very simple priority system. When it came to choosing, I came first, my work second, my physical environment third and my relationships fourth. I was truly selfish. Frequently, I would create arguments about choosing my work over my lover, or where I lived over my relationships. My priorities were clear, but they were hardly aligned with my heart's purpose.

For relationships to be all they can be, they must be your number one priority in life. Aside from your commitment to your own well-being and to God, nothing is as important as the people who love and support you. Do not take these people for granted. Relationships need nourishment and attention, or else they become automatic and your unconscious patterns have a field day.

Choosing your relationships over your work, home, hobbies and privacy is not a sacrifice; it's an affirmation that you value love over separation and that when your relationships are in order, your whole life works better. It wasn't until I chose love over work that my career, as well as my relationships, took off. Relationships are not opposed to careers; on the contrary, they provide the support, nourishment and inspiration to contribute more in the world. And the more you contribute, the more you extend friendship and loving relationships on the planet, which is the message of this book.

Business based on friendship is a healing force in the world. The more your business expands, the more Earth sees itself as a family business.

Home is the base from which you draw your love. The more you heal your relationship with your parents, the more love you can bring home. And the more healed you feel at home, the more you are able to share friendship at work. Your business relationships will get stuck at the same emotional points you are stuck with your family. Your boss will become your father, your co-workers your siblings.

So do yourself a favor. Go home!

Notes from My Journal

It was early September 1976. I was in Santa Fe, New Mexico. It was fiesta week. Everyone was drunk out of their minds. My marriage was on the rocks.

The highlight of fiesta is Zozobra, a huge puppet representing the god of gloom. Every year Zozobra is wired up in a huge field with hundreds and hundreds of people watching. Then he is electrocuted, and everyone cheers as mighty gloom bites the dust, overcome by the life force for one more year.

As I watched Zozobra burn, I felt my heart longing for some satisfaction that always seemed just beyond my grasp. I felt the loss, the defeat of divorce, the shame of separation. I cried as the smoke hit my eyes.

Soon I left Santa Fe and my wife. The day I left, our little white kitten "Egg" was hit by a truck but managed to haul his white bloody body back to our adobe house, where he died atop our king-sized bed, a red spot on a white bedspread. I didn't know then how pets often act out their master's death urge.

I was tired of the birth/death cycle of love and life. I felt hopeless, more despair than ever before, yet in the middle of my darkness was a seed of determination and certainty about which I felt very good.

"Never again!" I swore to myself. "Never again!"

It wasn't until I could be happy by myself that I could be happy with a woman.

After I split up with my wife, I did a lot of soul searching. An astrologer did my chart and told me I had a lot of Karma in the house of relationships. I didn't know much about Karma, but I knew I didn't feel at home in the house of relationships. In fact, I felt like a complete fool in matters of the heart.

And so I began to fool around a lot, thinking for awhile that the more relationships I had, the better I would get at them. Besides, I was addicted to sex.

Each affair was less satisfying than the previous one. I knew I was looking for something I could not find outside myself, but my behavior was so compulsive all I could do was notice how the more I sought for love outside myself, the deeper the pit within my gut felt. I was empty at the core. Alone. I was using sex to cushion me from my solitude. Only it wasn't working anymore.

Finally, in utter desperation, I chose to be celibate. It was the best thing I could have given myself. Almost immediately, the pressure lifted. I could see that I didn't even want sex anymore. That it was just a cover-up for my loneliness. What a relief!

That lasted about two days. Then I began to think there was something wrong with me. I should want sex. I would be even more alone if I didn't find someone to seduce, and fast! Women would forget about me completely! I would die, and no one would care! My mind was having a field day!

Weeks passed. I still had no desire. Months passed. I still was content to be alone. What the hell was wrong with me? Was I gay? Was I over the hill? What was the point of living without sex?

I was concentrating on my breathing one day when I suddenly saw that I had never really separated from my mother. Although I seemed like a totally independent person, on some energetic level I still needed a woman (i.e. my mother or some substitute) to empower me, as though there were a psychic umbilical cord going out from me to women, looking for an outlet to plug myself into.

I could see how I resented being dependent on women, how I had to destroy every relationship to prove that I didn't need a woman to survive, and how even that didn't work because the problem was in my mind and I couldn't seem to erase it.

Then one morning, I woke up, and the whole struggle had lifted. It was as if I had wrestled with the angel of death and won. I saw that my heart was open and that I loved a lot of women, and that love didn't mean automatic orgasm. I saw what friendship was, what love was and that I had run my sexual well dry out of fear and confusion. I realized for the first time in my life that I could be completely happy whether or not I ever had sex again.

Soon after that I met Mallie. How grateful I am that, explosive as the passion is between us, it is never compulsive. We are complete before we make love. Making love is gravy!

I remember the night I fell in love with the universe.

It was August, it was hot and I was driving West for the first time in my life. I had spent the first twenty-six years of my life in New York City. I was accustomed to vertical slabs of skyscrapers limiting my perception of sun and sky.

Driving through the Mojave Desert was something else. All that horizontal space just blew me away. I was, in my own mind, on another planet. I remember the night in Death Valley. There I was in the middle of the desert, in the middle of the universe, in the middle of nowhere, millions of stars shimmering like sparkling dust. I lay down on the floor of the universe and breathed it all in. Tears streamed down my face. It was an amazing experience, beyond any drug I had known. I lost all my boundaries, so that I could not feel where I began and the universe ended. It was all perfectly blended, inside and out, my lungs inhaling all of life and then, in turn, surrendering all of myself back into God.

Everything I thought I was dissolved at that moment. Everything I thought I knew about life disappeared. In that instant I knew for certain that I was safe, that life was good.

An all-pervasive sense of well-being flooded me. I was alive. I was in love with my life. And God's universe was a cosmic womb I could trust to nourish me.

My relationship with Mallie has always been extraordinary. Perhaps the most extraordinary thing about it is I still wake up every morning, look at her, and my mind is blown away by how much love my heart holds for her. This mind-blowing awakening seems to get worse every day, thank God.

I remember one of our first conversations. We were sitting on a couch and my heart was pumping like an oil well. I had promised myself I would never let my heart open like this again. I had had enough of up-and-down relationships. The peaks were no longer worth the valleys. I did not want to be feeling what I was feeling. I did not want a relationship. I was perfectly happy by myself, thank you. Quite frankly, I was terrified!

Suddenly Mallie said "I don't want a relationship," and I knew I had met my match.

"Neither do I!" I said, not really relieved.

"Well, then, I guess we don't have a problem."

"I guess not!"

But we did! Here we had this overwhelming love for each other. And, on the other hand, there was this deep mistrust of relationships. We had both been married previously, and for both of us marriage had proved to be a long drawn-out struggle. We had each had our share of flings, and that was more exhausting than exciting. We wanted something passionate but lasting. Unheard of!

It seemed to us that love was a no-win situation: Either we'd have a short passionate affair that would burn itself out, or a long boring relationship that would burn us out. Divorce, death or slow decay seemed our only models for love, and each alternative was entirely unacceptable to both of us.

But here was this undeniable love that just would not go away! What to do? For five days we sat on that couch, telling each other everything we hated about relationships, sharing all our fears and considerations. Every time I uttered a fear, I'd take a breath and relax, only to feel a new and more powerful wave of love overcome me. After five days the love seemed more immense than could be possible.

We decided then, in 1977, to become our own role models—to play with our relationship in a way we had never seen before and to devote ourselves to both excitement and longevity, two concepts we had never seen married in one relationship but which we were not willing to live without! And in all the years we have been together there has never been a moment I could call truly dull!

One of the most terrifying moments in my relationship with Mallie arrived after several months of living together. I woke up one morning and looked at my sleeping beauty, and tears came to my eyes. I felt so privileged to be sharing a bed with a woman so amazing, I had never slept with an angel before. She was the real thing!

Suddenly, fear gripped my throat and I could hardly breathe. A thought crossed my mind which was so staggering and confusing I didn't know what to do with it. The thought was: "I need her!"

You must understand that I was an enlightened being. I knew the difference between love and need, and I knew how devastating need could be to a loving relationship. I could feel my heart start to shut down. The fear of loss crept into every cell in my body. I was shaking!

Mallie and I had an agreement to tell the truth fast, but this one thought—"I need her"—would not come out in words. I was sure that the moment I expressed this thought, the bottom would drop out of my dream and I would be all alone. I remembered Werner Erhard saying, "the only reason we need someone is to have some-one to blame!"

For weeks I withheld expressing this thought. I watched Mallie from a distance for those days, and the lump in my throat felt like a time bomb that would inevitably explode.

Then one day I could not hold it in anymore. We were in the kitchen "Mallie," I said, my voice trembling, "I have something important to tell you." She turned to me. She smiled. (She always smiles!) At that moment she represented everything I ever wanted in a woman. And now I had to risk losing it. "I need you!" I blurted out. She laughed. "Is that it?" she said. "Well. I need you too!" We em-braced. My love for her surpassed itself.

Now I can see my folly clearly. The truth is, need is not a problem so much as the fear of need. Werner had it backwards. One of the main reasons we blame people is because we're afraid to tell them we need them! We're afraid to ask for help! The bottom line in any rela-tionship is that people don't really need each other. You survived previous to the relationship and surely you can survive another loss. Yet the closer we get to love, the more the memory of the cutting of the umbilical cord is (and the fear of reliving it) activated. We seek to stay in the womb of love for fear that if we come out into the world it will lead to loss.

This is called Special Relationships (see *A Course in Miracles*) and is best expressed by the thought "It's you and me, baby, against the world!" What has happened here is you have taken your personal fear of attack and loss and buried it under your partner's protection. Love becomes a shelter from the storm, a romantic Pentagon! Only it's a hopeless defense because the enemy is within.

I find that most relationships go through this cocoon stage. At some point you must choose to give up the world for your love, or so it seems. You have the right to bond with your mate. But Special Relationships that stay special eventually find the fate of Romeo and Juliet—a sweet death! At some point, for love to grow fully, it must come out and be shared with the world. At that point you have a Holy Relationship, based on inclusion, not exclusion.

We are all of us in need of each other. The world is a family of interdependent beings. To deny your needs, to protest your independence could be to protest too much!

To open your heart fully is to strive for self-sufficiency all the time, but, meanwhile, to be willing to share what you have, not hoard it, and, to acknowledge the interdependence of all life.

There is a natural ecology that governs the flow of love—if we could only get the dams of our minds out of the way.

So don't deny your feelings of neediness, helplessness and dependency. Denial keeps the energy stuck. Confession opens the heart!

The power of the mind never ceases to amaze me.

I remember a time, several years ago, when Mallie and I were experiencing feelings of separation in our relationship. We had just led a training in San Francisco and arrived at the airport for our return flight. When we got to the gate we were told that there were no adjacent seats available.

In all our years of traveling together, we had never experienced not being able to sit together on a plane. We always looked forward to this precious time alone. Airplanes were one of the few places we could be together without interruption—no doorbells, no telephones, no emergency clients.

Since we were enlightened, we immediately recognized that we were projecting our own thoughts of separation on this flight. It seemed ironic to us that we were flying on *United*, yet couldn't sit together. We walked away from the gate, looking for a solution instead of sulking (an alternative we've learned to reject).

Our belief is that every problem was once a solution to a previous problem. The separation we were feeling was clearly the result of having reached a level of intimacy that threatened our basic defense systems. Instead of using the problem to punish ourselves, we wandered through the airport mumbling "I love my separation, I love my separation" over and over again. We were simply accepting the problem as the solution. In the past we had had enormous success playing with the thought "I love my separation so much I'm willing to share it with everyone," which is quite a mind-bender. For now, "I love my separation" seemed to suffice.

Twenty minutes later, we returned to the gate; our energy felt good. "I love my separation. I love my separation." We were immediately informed that there were still no adjacent seats available. However, United would pay us $200 to take a flight that departed thirty minutes later, and we could sit anywhere we liked because that flight was practically empty. "Great!" we said, and walked off to the bar to celebrate our victory. Clearly, it pays to love your separation!

Mallie and I became so popular giving seminars that soon we outgrew our small apartment on West 106th Street. I remember one night talking to seventy people in our 13 x 18 living room. The subject was birth, and I was feeling very claustrophobic. We soon decided to move.

At the time, I was intellectually conscious of the relationship between birth and moving. I "knew" birth was the first big move of life and that all future transitions were experienced in the light of birth. I also "knew" it was not advisable for pregnant women to move into a new home. It was easy for me to understand this line of thinking. No problem at all.

It took nine months to find the perfect house. It wasn't *The New York Times* or *Village Voice* that did it either. It was utter hopelessness. One night I felt totally resigned to never getting out! We were stuck. There was no other place for us.

The next morning a real-estate agent who had gotten our number from another agent called. He had a place to show us. This was the one.

We were scheduled to move into our brownstone triplex the morning of July 1. The movers came, loaded the van and had us at our new doorstep before noon. We opened the door, only to discover the previous tenants in the midst of packing.

The long wait began. Frustration mounted. Hours passed. The rage and helplessness swelled up. The feelings were totally disproportionate to the situation. Okay, the old tenants were jerks. Okay, we had a lease to prove we had the right to move in. Okay, we had the right to be there. So what? The fact was, the jerks would be out by dusk and we'd be in. Still, it didn't feel all that certain; it felt like the cosmic rug had been pulled out from under us. It felt like Hell, or at least Limbo.

Knowing what we knew about birth, we had to look at our own minds. What was it in my primal subconscious scenario that I was projecting onto this move? I called my mother. I had already interrogated her fairly thoroughly about my birth, but every so often, in talking to her, a new piece of the puzzle would pop into place.

My mother answered the phone. I told her about the great moving delay and asked her about my birth. She reminded me about being born during the war, during a blizzard; how there was a shortage of hospital beds and nurses, how she was strapped down on a dolly, how the waiting seemed interminable and how finally the Father Divine nurses delivered me. I knew all this. I knew the anxiety of waiting inside out. Wasn't there something else?

Finally my mother told me. She had been moving into a new apartment the day she went into labor with me. The old tenants were slow in moving out. It was frustrating. The situation was the same. The feelings were the same. I could relax. The puzzle was a little clearer.

It still amazes me how precisely our lives imitate our births.

The truth about guilt hit me over the head one day.

I had understood the way guilt works: how all guilt is self-punishment and how self-punishment seeks agreement from the physical universe; how I could be guilty about failure or success; how I was not a victim; how all attack was just the result of the attack thoughts in my subconscious mind; how guilt was just my own personal mafia. I understood all this. (Like hell I did.)

The truth was, I could never comprehend how guilt worked until I unraveled one recurrent childhood memory. No matter how enlightened I became, the picture of Alan Goldstein sneaking up behind me and hitting me over the head with a baseball bat kept me stuck in victim mentality. What had I done to deserve that? Clearly, there were some things beyond my responsibility. Thank God. I could stay angry.

Then, one day while doing conscious breathing, the truth hit me over the head—the reason the baseball bat and my skull collided in time and space. I *had* been guilty. Alan Goldstein was the best baseball player; everyone knew that. But that fateful day I had played extremely well, better than Alan Goldstein, better than anyone. I had hit two home runs and made a spectacular catch. I remembered the feeling of exhileration after the game, and the uneasiness that followed. I could actually remember my thought at the time ("I'm not supposed to be that good!"), and I remembered the sound of the bat cracking against my head. I breathed, and screamed "I deserve to succeed!"

Suddenly I could feel in every cell of my body how and why the fear of success had always been greater than the fear of failure.

We are guilty creatures! We are more terrified of surpassing our family and friends than of landing on the moon. Why do so few of us succeed? We don't have the guts to risk getting hit over the head by baseball bats. At least that's my theory.

Song for Mallie

I always knew
how to fall in love;
I always knew
how to be in love;
but there is one thing
I never knew
until I found myself in you.

I never knew
how to stay in love;
I always thought
I had to pay for love;
I never found
my way in love
until I found my way to you.

I always knew
how to cry in love;
I even knew
how to die in love;
but there is one thing
I never knew
until the day I found you.

I never knew
how to be at home
with a love
I could call my own;
I always thought
I'd have to leave
until you showed me how to stay.

I always knew
how to make good love;
and when I didn't
I could fake good love;
but there is one thing
I never knew
until I made love to you.

I never knew
how to make love last;
I always thought
that love would pass;
I always made
my love so fast
until you showed me how to stay.

Open Heart Reminders

1. An open mind is the key to an open heart!
2. The beliefs you take to heart are the results you get in life!
3. An experience is the physical result of one or more thoughts.
4. Love is a powerful, life-supporting energy that flows through you when you flow through it.
5. It's safe to love again!
6. Every problem was once a solution to a previous problem.
7. What you can't feel, you can't heal.
8. Whatever comes up is on the way out.
9. Life never gives you more than you can handle.
10. Every feeling is a feeling of aliveness and, if not suppressed, will lead to greater love.
11. Fear is an invitation to greater safety with more energy.
12. Falling in love is feeling that the hopeless longing to have someone take care of you forever might finally be fulfilled.
13. The subconscious message in falling in love is "Catch me!"
14. Being in love is experiencing your lovable essence in the presence of someone.
15. Forgiveness is its own reward.
16. Jealousy is watching someone from whom you think you need attention give it to someone or something else.
17. You cannot bond with a mate until you set your parents free.
18. Guilt is the mafia of the mind.
19. Earth is a family business.
20. Freedom is the experience of choosing.
21. Peace is my passion!
22. I'd rather win love than arguments!
23. A stranger is someone with whom you feel strange.
24. The more grateful you are, the more you have to be grateful for.
25. Stop hiding from God.
26. You don't have to be a rebel to excel!
27. The only one you get even with is yourself.
28. Why struggle to earn the love you're already worth?

29. Angels fly high because they take themselves lightly.
30. Put your worst foot forward first.
31. The universe is still in creation.
32. Disapproving of others diminishes your self.
33. The more you take your time, the more time you have to take.
34. Slowly is holy.
35. Patience always outlasts hopelessness.
36. Your strength is stronger than your weakness.
37. Easy street is a good neighborhood.
38. Family means loving each other even when there's a difference of opinion.
39. You can only experience your infinite essence; your mind cannot measure the fullness of who you are.
40. All good relationships are grounded in friendship.
41. If you don't love yourself, who is supposed to do it for you?
42. Innocence can neither be created nor destroyed.
43. Rejection is an opportunity to love yourself more fully.
44. As you think of yourself, so you are thought of by others.
45. You can't find yourself by yourself.
46. People resist what they most desire.
47. Immortality is the master key: It opens the door to everything.
48. There is no scarcity.
49. There is more than enough for everyone to have more than enough.
50. You can have compassion without taking on people's pain.
51. A heart attack is an attack of heart!
52. Every upset is a set-up.
53. Intimacy means "into-me-see"!
54. All your feelings are valid.
55. You are already in possession of life's most precious possession, which is life itself.
56. Your body is the closest part of the physical universe to you.
57. You never lose anything that's for your highest good.
58. Whenever you seem to lose something of value, it's only to make room for something better.

59. Sometimes you have to fall apart in order to find out how together you really are.
60. God is the stars and the space between.
61. You don't have to be perfect to have a perfect relationship.
62. Saying no to what you don't want opens the door to what you do want.
63. You deserve to have it all!
64. Your life urge is stronger than your death urge!
65. Optimism is the philosophy of love and life.
66. Completion is a great place to start!

The Loving Relationships Training (LRT)

Much of the material in this book is supported and inspired by the LRT, a wonderful weekend workshop in loving relationships.

Created by Sondra Ray, author of *I Deserve Love* and *Loving Relationships,* the LRT is a turning point in many people's lives. In the seven years I have been associated with this training, I have witnessed thousands of transformations and healings. While a book such as this can be a valuable tool for re-connecting to yourself, you cannot finally find yourself by yourself. Your ego is so sneaky it can convince you of change where there is none. In the presence of an honest, enlightened group you are no longer able to fool yourself. The LRT is such a group, a conscious family where you unravel your problems and reveal your inherent magnificence. When you complete the weekend, you can never again pretend you don't know what's going on in your relationships. Moreover, you've had an unforgettable experience of your own self-esteem and the unlimited possibilities for all your relationships—at home, at work and at play.

The LRT restores fun, freedom and friendship to your life. It gives you a unique opportunity to replace compulsive behavior with spontaneous self-expression and to honor the love in your family while letting go of the negative aspects of our family tradition.

I have a T-shirt that says "Angels fly high because they take themselves lightly." The Loving Relationships Training is a workshop where you can laugh your way back home.

Contact Wendy McLeod at (212) 799-7324.

International Seminars Leadership Programs (ISLP)

ISLP offers a variety of extended personal growth programs for individuals and for couples.

The purpose of ISLP is to support conscious leadership in the world, a leader being an individual whose life is an inspiration to others. The programs, lasting from six weeks to six months, offer intensive support in breaking through family barriers that limit success in relationships and career, as well as in integrating these changes into your everyday life. In the course of a typical program you discover your purpose in life, your resistance to fulfilling that promise, and the deep drive you have to push that resistance out. The group supports you in releasing whatever is between you and participating in life fully.

Whether your intention is to create your ideal relationship, success at work, or both, ISLP can help you open your heart and have it all.

Contact Wendy McLeod at (212) 799-7324.

Professional Rebirthers

I heartily recommend the following Rebirthers (as of May 1, 1984).

New York

Peter and Meg Kane
34 West 85th Street, Apt. 1
NYC, NY 10024
(212) 580-8031

Robert & Doreen Marine
34 West 87th Street
NYC, NY 10024
(212) 877-7003

Gayle Carlton
145 West 87th Street
NYC, NY 10024
(212) 362-1172

Alex Lukeman
245 West 87th Street
NYC, NY 10024
(212) 362-1172

Judy Roberts
114 West 76th Street #BR
NYC, NY 10024
(212) 362-0083

Jane Klein
119 Payson Avenue
NYC, NY 10034
(212) 569-8598

Ron & Miri Gilad
342 West 85th Street #2B
NYC, NY 10024
(212) 595-1369

Wendy McLeod
125 West 85th Street
NYC, NY 10024
(212) 724-3652

Pennsylvania

Steve Clymer
Box 434
Pt. Pleasant, PA 18950
(215) 297-5552

Washington

Michael & Ila Shapiro
205 Yoakum Parkway #1504
Alexandria, VA 22304
(703) 370-1963

Emily Goldman
2226 River Road N.W.
Washington, D.C. 20016

Laura Harrison
8801 Maywood Avenue
Silver Spring, MD 20910
(301) 587-8237

Atlanta

Jim & Pru Collier
202 Ansley Villa Drive
Atlanta, GA 30324
(404) 233-3343

Barbara White
2850 Delk Rd., Apt. 54A
Atlanta, Georgia 30067
(404) 591-1636

Florida

Mikela Green
P.O. Box 537
N. Miami Beach, FL 33160
(305) 279-5882

Cincinnati

Karen Trennepohl
5074 Western Hills Ave.
Cincinnati, Ohio 45238
(513) 471-2410

Cindy Sefton
3438 Ferncroft Drive
Cincinnati, Ohio 45211
(513) 662-4978

Texas

Madeline Schaider
1407 Missouri, Suite 101
Houston, TX 77006
(713) 523-6419

Bobby Birdsall
1002 California, Garage Apt.
Houston, TX 77006
(713) 526-5317

Seattle

David & Doreen Tannenbaum
3705 E. John Street
Seattle, WA 98024
(206) 325-0745

California

Paul Laut
1636 N. Curson Avenue
Hollywood, CA 90046
(213) 876-6226

Linda Priest
13803 Valley Vista Blvd.
Sherman Oaks, CA 91423

Eve Jones
140 S. Norton
Los Angeles, CA 90004
(213) 461-5774

Rhonda Levand
1251 Fairburn Avenue
Los Angeles, CA 90024
(213) 470-4501

Manny Stamatakis
3406 Glendon Avenue #8
Los Angeles, CA 90034
(213) 202-0499

Leonard Orr
Campbell Hot Springs
P.O. Box 234
Sierraville, CA 96126
(916) 994-8984

Joe Moriarty
Campbell Hot Springs
P.O. Box 234
Sierraville, CA 96126
(916) 994-8984

Europe

Diana Roberts
Gillian Steel
Colne Denton
Old Ferry Wharf
Cheyne Walk
London SW10 England
D11 441 352 3977

Australia

Yvonne & Vincent Betar
44 Rae Street
Fitzroy North, Victoria 3068
Australia
61-3-481-5302

About the Author

Robert Steven Mandel is a graduate of Columbia College (B.A.) and Columbia Graduate Faculties (M.A.), where he studied philosophy, psychology and theatre. Mr. Mandel continued his post-graduate work at the Yale School of Drama, where he received the John Gassner Memorial Award for his writing and was assistant editor of "Yale/Theatre." Upon leaving Yale, Mr. Mandel moved to London where he was playwright-in-residence for The New Theatre. Returning to the states, his play "Sand Dwarfs" won him a National Endowment Award and he became an associate of Theatre Arts Corporation of New Mexico.

In 1976, Mr. Mandel's interest in the rehearsal process evolved into his concern with personal growth. For the last seven years he has worked extensively in the self-help field, as a Certified Rebirther, consultant, and creator of several trainings which he and his wife Mallie conduct around the country. In 1980, he founded ISLP, International Seminars Leadership Programs, and he has devoted much of his time to training people to break through to their own leadership potential.

Currently, Mr. Mandel is the National Director for the Loving Relationships Training, a popular weekend workshop given in the U.S.A., Canada and Europe. *Open Heart Therapy* is the result of seven years of research and work.